CONTEMPORARY EASTERN ORTHODOX THOUGHT
The Traditionalist Voice

Contemporary Eastern Orthodox Thought
THE TRADITIONALIST VOICE

by

ARCHIMANDRITE CHRYSOSTOMOS
with
HIEROMONK AUXENTIOS AND HIERODEACON AKAKIOS

1982
NORDLAND HOUSE PUBLISHERS
P.O. Box 452
Belmont Ma. 02178-0452
USA

Library of Congress Catalog Card Number 81-80112
ISBN 0-913124-54-0

© Copyright 1982 by
NORDLAND HOUSE PUBLISHERS

About the Author

The Very Rev. Dr. Chrysostomos is Abbot of the St. Gregory Palamas Monastery in Hayesville, Ohio, a small dependency of the Holy Monastery of Sts. Cyprian and Justina in Fili (Athens), Greece. A Princeton doctorate, he is Adjunct Assistant Professor of Christian Thought at Ashland Theological Seminary and Associate Professor of Psychology at Ashland College. His numerous scholarly writings have appeared in various theology and psychology journals in the US and abroad. He is the author of *The Ancient Fathers of the Desert* and *Orthodox Liturgical Dress*.

About the Contributors

Hieromonk Auxentios is Steward of the St. Gregory Palamas Monastery. He received his degree in religion from Princeton University and is a frequent contributor to Orthodox theological journals.

Hierodeacon Akakios graduated from the California State College, San Bernardino, and pursued graduate study at the University of California. An iconographer, he has contributed to scholarly journals in the social sciences and theology.

Contents

Acknowledgments

Were it not for the efforts of a number of people, this book would not have gone beyond the manuscript stage. For their technical skills, encouragement, and aid I owe a great debt of gratitude to the following: Dr. Charles Ferroni, Mrs. Barbara McGovern, Dr. Naomi Saslow, all of Ashland College, Mrs. Virginia Ferroni, Helen Lutz, and Mr. and Mrs. George Chapman, Jr.

The late Protopresbyter Georges Florovsky, while we were both at Princeton University, first suggested that I write a book of this kind. Dr. Constantine Cavarnos, of Hellenic College and the Institute for Byzantine and Modern Greek Studies, kindly reviewed several essays in the book and has been a source of scholarly and personal support. The Very Rev. Dr. N. Michael Vaporis, Professor and Dean at Hellenic College and Director of the Holy Cross Orthodox Press, has contributed much to my work. I would like to make the occasion of the publication of this book a statement of my appreciation for the kindness of these three dedicated men.

All of the ideas in this book have reference to the Orthodox spiritual life and thus to my own development in that sense. The friendship of three outstanding thinkers helped me bring the worlds of spirit and mind closer together. I must, then, thank Dr. Jeffrey Russell, of the University of California, Santa Barbara, Dr. Nikolai Khokhlov, and Dr. Lee Kalbus, both of the California State College, San Bernardino. Mother Alexandra, Abbess of the Orthodox Monastery of the Transfiguration (in Ellwood City, Pennsylvania) and former Princess of Rumania, has contributed, by her example, gentility, and kindness, more to my spiritual life than she perhaps knows. Of similar importance have been the advice and direction of my spiritual seniors, the Fathers of the St. Herman of Alaska Monastery (in Platina, California).

Finally, my spiritual Father, Bishop Cyprian, himself the spiritual son of Archimandrite Philotheos (Zervakos) of late and blessed memory, is my foundation. Without his guidance, peril awaits me at every turn in my spiritual life. May the inadequacy of my work not reflect on the excellence of his paternal advice and direction.

ARCHIMANDRITE CHRYSOSTOMOS
Feast of St. Gregory Palamas
Nov. 14, 1980 (Old Style)

Introduction

In the past few decades, Western Christians, scholars and the simple faithful alike, have come to understand and appreciate the Eastern Orthodox Church more than ever before. With increasing frequency, Americans and Western Europeans encounter Orthodox immigrants living their faith in the West and westerners who have embraced Orthodoxy through conversion. In the United States, for example, Orthodox Christians are no longer a small minority of people practicing a strange religion imported from Greece, Russia, Rumania, Bulgaria, and the Middle East. They are now recognized as those millions of Americans who adhere to what the popular Time-Life series on the great religions of the world has called "Christianity's oldest Church." In the Eastern Orthodox religion, which immigrants brought to the West with them, westerners are discovering the "other half of Christianity," an ancient Christian witness which faded in the western consciousness after its estrangement from the East.

A Roman Catholic prelate of the Byzantine Rite recently noted that the Gospels, the Pauline Epistles, the great ecumenical councils of the early Church, the Christian liturgies (including those of ancient Rome), many of the greatest Fathers and Doctors of the Church, and, indeed, monasticism are essentially eastern in origin. They came from the East and their media of expression were largely Greek and other eastern tongues. It is no wonder, then, that the West has discovered the Orthodox Church. In a sense, it has discovered its own past—its own roots. So it is that many general surveys of the Eastern Orthodox Church and its unique Christian witness have become popular in the West. One need only mention Archimandrite

Kallistos (Timothy) Ware's excellent little volume, *The Orthodox Church,* now in its tenth printing, to characterize the popularity of these texts. They have given non-Orthodox, Western Christians some notion of the inner life and spirit of the Christian East.

As Western Christians discover the Orthodox Church and its singular witness, Eastern Orthodox living in the West are also beginning to find new dimensions in their faith. For, indeed, Orthodox themselves have, in many ways, much to discover about their past. While the West has reached a kind of cultural ascendancy in the past few centuries, the East has seen its culture attacked, transformed by outside forces, and subjected to brutal captivity. Constantinople, the historical spiritual and political center of Eastern Orthodox Christendom, now enters its fifth century of domination, which began with the Moslem destruction of the Byzantine Empire in the fifteenth century. Orthodox Christians in the Middle East and Greece, the spiritual cradle of Eastern Christianity, have seen but a few decades of peace in the last two centuries. And in the present century, the giant Orthodox empires of Eastern Europe have fallen, one by one, to the hostile force of communism. In such circumstances, it is not surprising that, though not a few have lived and died with valor for their faith, a great many Orthodox have lost much of the richness of their tradition. The demands of survival precede those of acute self-knowledge.

If Orthodox, too, have gained from the revival of interest in the Christian East among westerners, there have been some costs. When one rediscovers his own past through the eyes of others, that past is subtly changed. Thus, many Orthodox see their faith through the eyes of those who do not share their past, through the words and images of western expositors whose conceptual framework is non-Orthodox. A few decades ago, more Orthodox than one would care to think were content to accept themselves as would-be Roman Catholics who maintained a married clergy and eschewed the notion of papal supremacy. Others saw their faith as a kind of theological compromise between Roman Catholicism and Protestantism.

However uncomfortable these Orthodox might have ultimately been with such characterizations, they more often than not lacked the vocabulary to express their unique positions and traditions in any other way. They became the unwilling captives of the alien categories and conceptions by which westerners had attempted to explain Orthodoxy to themselves.

Further complicating the problem of accurate self-knowledge and self-presentation for Orthodox in the West has been the unique experience of Byzantine Catholics in the United States. Many such Catholic immigrants, finding their married clergy and Byzantine traditions (generally respected by the Latin hierarchy in Europe) unacceptable to the Roman Catholic Church in the US, fled to various Orthodox jurisdictions. (It is estimated that seventy-five percent of the forefathers of present members of one of the larger Orthodox jurisdictions in the US, the Orthodox Church of America, were formerly Byzantine Catholics. The entire Carpatho-Russian Orthodox Church in America was once Byzantine, or Greek, Catholic.) For these Orthodox, understanding their new faith through western eyes was not a loss of some unique vision, as with native Orthodox; it was an unavoidable and necessary consequence of their own past. One large segment of the Orthodox Church in the West, therefore, encouraged a view of Orthodoxy which had its roots in a referential scheme. They could best understand Orthodoxy not through a comparative approach, which emphasized its unique and separate witness vis-à-vis western theological traditions, but only as Orthodoxy could be grasped in reference to the problems and issues with which they were familiar.

In reaction to this discovery of Orthodoxy by way of constant reference to western theological issues, there has arisen a countertrend, also several decades in progress, among Orthodox scholars. This trend emphasizes the growth of self-knowledge among Eastern Orthodox, not by a referential approach, but by investigating the Orthodox witness as it stands alone amidst the particular theologic issues and concerns which have shaped it—not as a witness somewhere between Roman Catholicism and Protestantism, but as a separate tradition with unique concerns that can be traced back to the concerns of the Fathers of the early Church. Some have, therefore, called this trend a "Patristic Revival," the "Hellenization" of contemporary theology (i.e., a conscious return to the Greek patrimony in which Orthodox Christian thought was born), or simply "traditionalism." For, to be sure, if Orthodoxy is anything, it is the traditional voice of the Church Fathers, the consensus of the ancients resounding in our times. And what is the Church, to the Orthodox Christian, but the Truth which the Fathers protected, the Apostles preached, and Christ himself delivered?

For some time now, I have felt the need for a volume of essays that touch on Eastern Orthodoxy from the standpoint of its own self-conception; indeed, from the "traditionalist" standpoint, in the spirit of the "Patristic Revival." Both in lecturing and teaching at a seminary and in a college, I and other colleagues have found it possible to bring the Orthodox witness to non-Orthodox students by way of the various introductory surveys available and in a general, referential context. Our students have come to know, for example, how Orthodox view faith and good works in reference to the views of various Protestant and Roman Catholic writers on the subject. They come to understand the seven sacraments as the Orthodox see them, and come to an all-too-limited apprehension of how the Orthodox position contrasts with the positions of the western confessions. One suspects that many Orthodox, attempting to understand and capture their own beliefs, know little more of their faith than these students.

But what of the true comparative approach? What of the pure Orthodox view itself? In fact, Orthodox theologians have never greatly concerned themselves with what they consider the artificial odds at which westerners place faith and good works. To understand these issues in an Orthodox context is to turn from western theological problematics to an entirely unique and separate mentality that has no direct counterpart in Roman Catholic and Protestant thought. The sacraments, or, more precisely, the mysteries, were never so carefully catalogued and enumerated, as in the West, until Orthodox theologians were forced, in their encounters with the West, to speak in alien terms. To speak of Orthodox mysteries by reference to western sacraments is to lose the essence of the Orthodox view. To compare the unique eastern view of the mysteries with the separate western view of the sacraments is a far more fruitful and appropriate approach. In the true comparative approach, Orthodoxy must be seen in terms of its own priorities and traditions, as it sees itself when freed from western conceptual schemata. This small book is a humble contribution to the growing number of works dedicated to fulfilling the need for such a vision.

There is a specific arrangement in the essays presented. I believe that they allow the reader to encounter a variety of issues in Orthodox thought from the standpoint of Orthodox traditionalism, while at the same time affording an opportunity to see the faulty consequences of a referential approach. The first essay attempts to distinguish the categories of thought and the spiritual goals of Eastern Orthodox Christianity from those of Western Christianity—to see man, the world, salvation, and even God in a uniquely Orthodox way. The second essay traces some of the historiographical prejudices that led western scholars to a loss of knowledge about the Christian East. In the third chapter, the reader finds a vivid contrast of the eastern and western views of Scripture and tradition, with a deliberate focus on the unique position of the Orthodox Church regarding these issues. In the following two chapters, there is an effort to summarize the problem of referential approaches to Eastern Orthodox thought (specifically as that problem is encountered in the western treatment of the hesychastic tradition), showing both the limitations of a referential approach and the richness of an approach recognizant of the unique character of Orthodox thought.

Chapter six is an exhortation of sorts, warning Eastern Orthodox in America of the limited and inaccurate self-understanding that results from viewing the Church in western categories and outside the spiritual milieu in which Orthodoxy has been transmitted from generation to generation. The seventh chapter continues the theme of chapter six, emphasizing that Orthodoxy has not only a spiritual culture, but a social culture, a singular ethos in which Orthodoxy is also transmitted. In chapter eight, the reader finds clear evidence of the plurality of views that constitutes Eastern Orthodoxy and some indication of the dimensions of the paucity of self-knowledge that besets Orthodoxy in the West and, indeed, in traditional Orthodox countries themselves. The last essay is a clear indictment of the inadequacy of the imposition of alien, western standards on Eastern Orthodoxy as a means to any rational understanding of her witness and antiquity.

1

Notes on the Nature of God, the Cosmos, and *Novus Homo*: An Eastern Orthodox Perspective

by

HIEROMONK AUXENTIOS

The Orthodox Church approaches theology in quite a different manner than the Western Church. If one keeps in mind the oft-cited maxim of St. Athanasios that God became man that man might become divine, the Orthodox view of theology is not difficult to grasp. And it is precisely the perspective grasped in that maxim that is the sine qua non for understanding the Orthodox stance vis-à-vis God, the cosmos, and the "new man." To approach these subjects without considering the unique theological dialectic of the Eastern Church would be unwise indeed.

The Holy Apostle Paul wrote various letters that have for many hundreds of years been recognized by the Church as "inspired." They are recognized as such not because of St. Paul's own special worth, but rather because of the divinity which dwelled within him. "I have been crucified with Christ; it is no longer I who live, but Christ who lives in me" (Gal. 2:20). St. Paul's resurrected condition is a potential offered to every Christian. Also, the Holy Spirit still bestows his gifts, allowing men to witness and serve with wisdom, knowledge, faith, discernment, and miracles (1 Cor 12:8-10). Therefore, a man's words still may be "inspired," but not because of his own aptitudes, rationality, intelligence, or any other quality specific to man's own nature, but because God dwells within him. The indwelling divinity literally transforms a man and gives a completely new life to the old, death-ridden nature. It is then that human actions, faculties, and words correctly serve

"Notes on the Nature of God, the Cosmos, and *Novus Homo*: An Eastern Orthodox Perspective" originally appeared in the *Greek Orthodox Theological Review* 21:3 (1976) 251-264. Reprinted by permission.

the immanent and ineffably transcendent God. Here we have the *Ursprung* of Orthodox theology.

For the Eastern Orthodox Church, then, the most highly regarded theologians, the theologians *pleno jure*, are those who have died that Christ might live within them. They are men who have been transformed by the fulness of God's grace, who have basked in the glory of his mysteries, and who speak from what they have seen. They are holy or, as the West would have it (and limitingly so),[1] mystics. Because of the divinity which fills these men, they can do nothing but reflect and affirm the words of Christ and the Apostles. For "Jesus Christ is the same yesterday and today and for ever" (Heb 13:8). The Holy Fathers may differ in style and sometimes even in nomenclature, but at the deepest and most authentic level they and the Apostles are stating together the same thing, affirming the one truth, the "mystical theology."

Such "mystical theology" is of no small importance for the Orthodox Church. It is not aloof or speculative; it is inextricably involved in the whole of church life. As are the Holy Gospels, the writings of the Fathers are invaluable milestones and guideposts for each soul's ascent to its Creator. Equally important, these writings safeguard and embody the purity and tradition of the Church, which, in her divinely appointed forms of worship and communion, offers the soul-transforming, grace-filled food. The Divine Liturgy itself is permeated with the teachings of the Fathers, as the Fathers are filled with the same grace of the Liturgy. All this is because "in these last days he has spoken to us by a Son" (Heb 1:2), because God has freely offered his transforming grace to men, who on their own chose (and merited) perdition. God, the cosmos, the "new man" cannot be understood outside of the mystical theology which lives and breathes this "transforming grace."

(1) For a discussion of the frequently improper usage of the term "mystic," especially as applied to the practitioners of hesychasm, see John S. Romanides, "Notes on the Palamite Controversy and Related Topics—II," *Greek Orthodox Theological Review* 9:2 (1963-1964), esp. p. 230.

The Nature of God. A proper understanding of the nature of God is important for at least two reasons. First, it is God whom man seeks in his activities, the God who sought man first (Staretz Silouan). It is, therefore, important that man be properly directed in all aspects of his search, lest he fall short of the True God in his worship, prayers, or aspirations. Secondly, man himself is made in the image of God, and it is only in his relationship to God that he comes to understand his own true nature. To know the purpose and function of the pot, one has to know something about the potter.

Paradoxically, God is ultimately unknowable. The greatest depths of his nature and essence will remain inaccessible to man forever.

> The superessential nature of God is not a subject for speech or thought or even contemplation, for it is far removed from all that exists and more than unknowable, being founded on the uncircumscribed might of the celestial spirits—incomprehensible and ineffable to all forever.[2]

To safeguard the doctrine of God's ultimate transcendence of human cognition, Orthodoxy makes a hierarchical distinction between "cataphatic" and "apophatic" theologies, which correspond in type to theological affirmations or denials, respectively. Cataphatically, God is an ultimate and eternal Being; on the higher and more "truthful" apophatic level, however, God is not in essence understandable by terms like ultimate, eternal, or Being. God is, in the apophatic sense, beyond levels of gradation and beyond the categories of time and existence themselves, since these are but categories appropriate to mere human thinking. Saint Dionysios the Areopagite, whose short treatise *Concerning Mystical Theology* is a prototypical exposition of the higher road of apophatic theology, concludes, strangely enough, with a denial of denial itself:

> When we make affirmations and negations about the things which are inferior to it (God), we affirm and

---

(2) St. Gregory Palamas, *Theophanes*, PG 150:937.

deny nothing about the Cause itself, which, being
wholly apart from all things, is above all affirmation,
as the supremacy of Him who, being in His simplicity
freed from all things and beyond everything, is above
all denial.[3]

All categories of human thought and apprehension fall radically short of the Godhead.

The fact that Dionysios chose "Concerning Mystical Theology" as the title for his treatise on the preeminence of apophatic theology is indicative of the practical importance of theology. The apophatic way, "Mystical theology," is, upon internalization, a disposition of the mind and soul that keeps one from being shackled either by his own mode of apprehension (God being beyond apprehension) or by any object of contemplation (God being beyond subject-object distinctions). Its aim is precisely the aim of the rest of Christianity: participation in and union (albeit limited) with the Godhead. Thus, apophaticism is at the heart of the formulation of Christian dogma, of the mysteries of revelation.

Negative theology is not merely a theory of ecstasy. It
is an expression of that fundamental attitude which
transforms the whole of theology into a contemplation
of the mysteries of revelation. . . . Apophaticism teaches
us to see above all a negative meaning in the dogmas
of the Church: it forbids us to follow natural ways of
thought and to form concepts which would usurp the
place of spiritual realities. For Christianity is not a philosophical school for speculating about abstract concepts, but is essentially a communion with the living
God.[4]

The doctrine of the Holy Trinity is yet another doctrine that is apophatic at heart. Orthodox dogma teaches that the Godhead is made up of three distinct persons (hypostases), with the ful-

(3) PG 3:1048.

(4) Vladimir Lossky, *The Mystical Theology of the Eastern Church* (London: James Clarke and Co., 1957), p. 42.

ness of the divine nature residing in each person: one nature *(homoousios)* residing equally in three persons *(hypostases)*.

> When I speak of God you must be illumined at once by one flash of light and by three. Three in Properties or Hypostases . . . but One in respect of the *ousia*—that is, the Godhead. For they are divided indivisibly, if I may say so; and they are conjoined dividedly. For the Godhead is One in Three, and the Three are One, in whom the Godhead is, or, to speak more accurately, Who are the Godhead.[5]

The Godhead is "indivisibly divided" or distinguished into three persons on the basis of origin. The Father is the unbegotten or ungenerated, the Son is begotten of the Father, and the Holy Spirit proceeds from the Father; yet, each of them bears the fulness of the divine nature. The "how" of the Son's begottenness or of the Holy Spirit's procession is a mystery that is simply unavailable to human understanding.

> You ask, what is the procession of the Holy Spirit? Do you tell me first what is the unbegottenness of the Father, and I will then explain to you the physiology of the generation of the Son, and the procession of the Spirit, and we will both of us be stricken with madness for prying into the mystery of God.[6]

The oneness of the Godhead is preserved by the monarchy of the Father, who is the sole source of divine nature. Yet, as noted previously, the divine nature resides wholly and equally in each of the three persons:

> Godhead . . . neither increased nor diminished by superiorities or inferiorities; in every respect equal, in every respect the same (save the distinctions of origin—unbegotten, begotten, proceedings; . . . the infinite connaturality of Three Infinite Ones, each God when considered in himself; as the Father so the Son, as the Son so the Holy Ghost; the Three, one God when

---

(5) St. Gregory Nazianzen, *In Sancta Lumina, Oratio XXXIX* 11, PG 36:345.
(6)Idem, *Oratio XXXI (Theologica V)* 8, PG 36:146.

5

contemplated together, each God because consubstantial; the Three, one God because of the monarchy.[7]
Thus there is a perfect balance in Orthodox dogma between the threeness and the oneness of God.

The Holy Fathers take special pains to preserve the paradox of the Trinity, for it is not a doctrine subject to human consideration; rather, the Holy Trinity is eternally at the heart of the Godhead, regardless of man's activity or existence. It was only by revelation that man learned of that which was eternally so, without cause. Therefore, the doctrine of the Holy Trinity is proper to an apophatic disposition, for man of himself can neither produce, nor rationalize, nor comprehend the fact that three equals one in the Godhead. In order to participate in this mystery, man must relinquish those operations proper to himself and immerse himself in that which has come from beyond.

Apophaticism finds its fulfillment in the revelation of the Holy Trinity as primordial fact, ultimate reality, first datum which cannot be deduced, explained, or discovered by way of any other truth, for there is nothing which is prior to it. Apophatic thought, renouncing every support, finds its support in God, whose incomprehensibility appears as Trinity. Here thought gains a stability which cannot be shaken, theology finds its foundation; ignorance passes into knowledge.[8]

The Cosmos. The Orthodox understanding of the cosmos also has its foundation in revelation and consequently has a predominantly soteriological (and theocentric) orientation: ''I beseech you, my child, to look at the heaven and the earth and see everything that is in them, and recognize that God made them out of things that did not exist. Thus also mankind comes into being'' (2 Macc 7:28). The creation was *ex nihilo,* out of nothing. Before the creation nothing existed outside of God. There was no formless matter upon which he imposed order and form; all levels of creation, from the grossly physical to the

(7) Idem, *In Sanc. Bapt., Oratio XL* 43, PG 36:417.
(8) Lossky, p. 64.

6

spiritually angelic, were called forth by God from nothingness. Thus, creation has no ontological source—rather it has nothingness for a nonontological source. Again, creation was not an outpouring of the divine nature. God remained separate from his creation, or the creation existed outside God, not geometrically but by the difference in the uncreated and created natures. "All things are from God; not in place, but in nature." [9]

As regards the cause of the creation, Orthodoxy is careful to assert that the creation was a *free* act of God.

> God contemplated all things before their existence, formulating them in his mind; and each being received its existence at a particular moment, according to his eternal thought and will, which is predestination, an image and a model. [10]

The divine ideas, the "thought-wills" or "predestinations" of God, do not in any way determine God's essence. They are dynamic and intentional in character, and thus have their place in his energies, not in his essence (the uncreated, divine energies being a part of the uncreated nature of God but distinct from the forever inaccessible essence of God). [11] There is thus no link of necessity between the divine nature and the creation. God did not "have to" create, nor is his creation by any necessity a replica of his own divine nature. Rather, his creation is entirely fresh and has been granted existence (out of nothingness) by a free, noncontingent act of his own will.

Just as creation had its cause in the free will of God, so too all of creation must look to God for a meaning and purpose to its existence. Created being was from its very inception made for change. All of creation came into being according to the corresponding divine ideas which preordained, or modeled, the different mode of each creature's participation in the uncreated energies. Instead of immediately realizing this foreordained participation (which would have made the creation less a creative

---

(9) St. John of Damascus, *Writings,* tr. Frederic H. Chase, Jr. (New York: Fathers of the Church, Inc., 1958), p. 199.

(10) Idem, *De fide orthodoxa* 2, PG 94:837.

(11) After Lossky, p. 95.

act of a personal God and more the simple effluence of the divine nature), each creature was offered a path of "synergy," wherein the created will should cooperate with the divine "idea-willings" of God in the process of deification, the increased participation in (the uncreated energies of) the Godhead. Therefore, deification is the end and meaning of creation, implicit in its very beginning.

The Eastern tradition knows nothing of "pure nature" to which grace is added as a supernatural gift. For it, there is no natural or "normal" state, since grace is implied in the act of creation itself.[12]

Man's Divinely Appointed Function and His Fall. Man, in his diversity, participates in all levels of created being. Within himself he finds elements of the "intelligible universe" (the realm of knowledge and angelic spirits) as well as of the "sensible universe" (the world that we perceive through our five senses). By uniting these diverse elements within himself—thus uniting the whole of creation—and simultaneously surrendering himself unto God "in a complete abandonment of love,"[13] man would have expressed the willful self-offering of the whole of creation unto the Creator. God, in his turn, would have given himself unto man, and thus effected the deification of the whole of his creation in and through his last creature (man.) This is the potential, the divinely appointed function that was given to man.

But man failed in his task. His failure was one of disobedience, a lapsing out of the cooperation implied in "synergy," a setting up of his own will against that of God. For Orthodox, man's fall, the *lapsus,* was like a wayfarer departing from the path, indeed the only path, that led to his rightful home. The fall was not a departure from an originally static and perfect nature; it was the interruption—the cessation of a priceless process. Thus the consequences of the fall were not products of what man had lost, but of what he had chosen. Man did not lose his

(12) Ibid., p. 101.
(13) Ibid., p. 110.

free will; he chose to exercise his will outside and even against that of his Creator, which necessarily weakened his own will and restricted its scope. Man did not "fall" into a state where his nature became sinful. He chose to remain and indulge in his own undeified nature, refusing the grace (and concomitant deification) that God offered. The consequence of man's denial of interior grace was slavery. Man became a "slave to sin," a state wherein he could not bridge the separation, or rather reopen the bridge he had denied between himself and God. Note that sin is not here (or anywhere else in Orthodoxy) a succumbing to something that is intrinsically evil; instead, sin is a willful participation in any activity in such a manner as to separate oneself from God.

Hence, as man approaches Christ he comes as a somewhat crippled creature, not as one thoroughly destroyed. His fall was not from the heights of heaven, but from a precious road; so, man "is not to be judged too harshly for his error"[14] (though the denial of his potential is indeed lamentable). His free will is restricted in scope, but by no means wholly lost. "The image of God is distorted by sin, but never destroyed. . . ."[15] Such an understanding of the fall—from a process, not a state, and with the retention of the "image"—will be seen below to correspond to the Orthodox hesychastic tradition, the renewal of divinization made possible by Christ.[16]

The Incarnation and Hesychasm. In any discussion of the incarnation, man must be careful not to lavish layers of human dependencies or categories upon what was wholly a divine revelation. Even to speak of this great mystery in the syllogisms of mundane logic is to distort it. In this respect, Ernst Benz, contrasting Orthodox and western theology, has remarked upon

(14) Timothy Ware, *The Orthodox Church* (Baltimore: Penguin Books, 1963), p. 228.

(15) Ibid., pp. 228-29.

(16) The importance of this possibility of divinization for the hesychastic tradition is made quite clear in a parenthetical footnote in Archimandrite Chrysostomos' "History and Politics of the Byzantine Church." See below, chapter 2.

9

the excesses of the Western Church:

> While Paul's doctrine of justification never had any decisive importance in the East, . . . it had far-flung consequences for the West. . . . Anselm of Cantebury (1033-1109) viewed the legal relationship existing between God and man as the very cornerstone of all theological thinking, so much so that he believed he could logically deduce the truth of the Christian religion and the necessity for the incarnation of God from the idea of "satisfaction." The covenantal theology of scholasticism regarded the history of salvation in general as a history of ever-renewed legal covenants between God and man.[17]

As with the creation of the very cosmos, man must not attribute any "necessity" to God's actions. Such anthropomorphizing in logical categories is a hindrance to true theological understanding.

In keeping with any of God's actions, the incarnation must first and foremost be understood as an act of love: "For God so loved the world that he gave his only Son, that whoever believes in him should not perish but have eternal life" (John 3:16). The Fathers of the Church have restated this "Gospel in miniature" countless times: "For he was made man, so that we might be made God."[18] The act of incarnation as well as the content (Christ) proceeds from the depths or heart of God, because it corresponds to his very nature—love (1 John 4:8). Because of the unfathomable depth from which the incarnation proceeds, man with his limited view can offer no truer (or more accurate) explanation than "love." Therefore, instead of dealing with the "why" or "how," the Fathers of the Church (following the example of the Gospels) address their attention to the effects of the incarnation.

(17) Ernst Benz, *The Eastern Orthodox Church: Its Thought and Life*, tr. Richard and Clara Winston (Garden City, N.Y.: Anchor Books, 1963), p. 46.

(18) St. Athanasios, *On the Incarnation of the Word*, in Phillip Schaff and Henry Wace, eds., *Nicene and Post-Nicene Fathers*, vol. 4 (Grand Rapids: Eerdmans, 1957), p. 65.

From man's fallen point of view, the incarnation immediately means a deliverance from the bonds of sin.

What is new in the New Testament . . . is the Incarnation and salvation event whereby the power of the devil is abolished once and for all, and the Body of Christ, the Church, is delivered from death (Hades) and made inviolate against its gates.[19]

When we spoke of man's fall, we mentioned that the consequences of man's willful departure from "synergy" were a rejection of the interior working of grace and a subsequent bondage to sin. From another point of view, man's fall is viewed as an arrogant assumption of roles proper only to God. Though he had apart from God no true life within himself, man chose to view the world as though he himself were a lord and the creator. His perception of the world "fell" and became appropriately conformed to his fallen self-image. For example, according to his "creator" image, man began to think that he himself was the creator of the highest expression of life—his children (a delusion, for only God creates life, being the Way, Truth, and Life himself). Or, according to his "lord" image, man came to view the world as having been created solely for his own pleasure and dominion. Having isolated himself from the grace of God, he became entrapped in his illusory self-worldview, which came to bear less and less resemblance either to the real world (and its corresponding potential) or to the "image" within him (and the corresponding potential of "likeness," of becoming divine).[20] Thus, in addition to isolation from interior grace, a blindness to man's (and the world's) true potential and a bondage to the illusory self-view (and worldview)

---

(19) Romanides, p. 249.

(20) On the idea of "likeness," Ouspensky cites the first mention of man in Scripture—"Let us make man according to our image and likeness" (Gen 1:26)—and remarks: "According to this design, man should be not only an image of God, his Creator, but should also bear his likeness. Yet in the description of the accomplished act of creation 'And God made man, according to the image of God he made him' (Gen 1:27), nothing is said about likeness. It is given to man as a task, to be fulfilled by the action of the Holy Spirit, with the free participation of man himself." Leonid Ouspensky and Vladimir Lossky, *The Meaning of Icons* (Boston, 1956), p. 35.

11

are proper descriptions of the result of the fall.[21]

From such an understanding of the fall, the deliverance from the bonds of sin ("whereby the power of the devil is abolished once and for all") is seen as occurring through the gift of a new vision to man. This is the vision of a renewed potentiality, or likeness, offered by God—in Christ—to man. Christ, the second Adam, showed man what the true likeness of God was, and at the same time he bore the means—grace—to that end. Christ (perfect man) was not only God's message to man of what he might be, but was also the uncreated divinity who transforms (perfect God); Christ was (indeed, *is*) the Word.

Orthodox, looking from a human perspective (obviously limited), view the incarnation as a radical intrusion of God into man's fallen world,[22] an "expression" of God's love for man and intense "desire" to return the lost sheep to the fold[23] before its (man's) perdition was sealed. At the same time, Eastern Orthodox see the depth of love within that "intrusion," where God humbled himself to an infinite degree in order to speak to man in his own language and to attract his willful participation in the soteriological scheme.[24]

But perhaps the best understanding of the incarnation (or any subject of theology) can be seen in the hesychastic tradition of "noetic prayer," which is regarded by the Orthodox Church as the highest form of prayer. The words "Lord Jesus Christ, Son of God, have mercy on me a sinner," or a slight variant thereof, usually constitute the verbal component of the prayer; but as simple as these words may seem, the theology behind the prayer is endless. For our purpose suffice it to say that for

(21) The illusory nature of man's *Weltansicht* is beautifully presented by Bishop Ignaty Brianchaninov in his response to man's "normal" worldly experience: "Beloved brother, the peace which makes you think your way is right is simply insensitivity and unawareness of your sinfulness due to your negligent life, while the joy you feel from time to time as a result of outward success and human praise is not holy and spiritual joy at all; it is the fruit of self-opinion, self-satisfaction, and vainglory." This translated excerpt from Bishop Ignaty's *The Arena* can be found in an excellent editorial essay: "A Man Is His Faith," *Nikodemos* 4 (1975) 12.

(22) This concept of intrusion is implied in John 1:14.

(23) See John 10:11f and Matt 18:10f.

(24) St. Athanasios, *Incarnation of the Word*, esp. section 41.

12

the words of the prayer itself:

> Far from rendering the interior life mechanical, [they
> have] the effect, on the contrary, of freeing it and turning
> it towards contemplation ["making it receptive to di-
> vinization" is truer to Orthodoxy] by constantly driving
> away from the region of the heart all contagion of sin,
> and every external thought or image; and this by the
> power of the most holy Name of Jesus.[25]

Before dealing with the transformation of man that is the
aim of hesychasm, a brief statement of Orthodox anthropology
is necessary. Man is basically bipartite, with a soul, composed
of a noetic faculty (*nous*—often translated as "spirit") and a
discursive intellect (sometimes replaced by *psyche*), and a body.
The noetic faculty is capable of interaction with both the soul's
discursive intellect and the physical body, and a reordering of
this interactive relationship is precisely the effect of the incarnation.[26]

According to hesychastic tradition:

> The noetic faculty is liberated by the power of the Holy
> Spirit from the influences of both the body and the
> discursive intellect and engages uninterruptedly and
> ceaselessly with prayer alone. The fascinating thing
> about this actual state of prayer . . . is that, although
> the physical and intellectual faculties no longer exercise
> any influence whatsoever on the noetic faculty, they are
> themselves, however, dominated by the noetic faculty's
> unceasing prayer in such a fashion that they are spir-
> itually cleansed and inspired and at the same time may
> engage in their normal activities.[27]

The awakening of the noetic faculty is the precise work of the
incarnation. Christ broke man's bondage to his (man's) fallen
view of the world ("the influences of both the body and the
discursive intellect") by restoring within him the vision of the
potential to which he was called. At the same time Christ gave

(25) Lossky, pp. 210-11.
(26) Romanides, p. 229.
(27) Ibid.

the means by which man could *realize* his "liberation" from bondage—the Comforter, ". . . the power of the Holy Spirit," grace. This power, grace, is what might be called the God-given language that is appropriate to the reactivated noetic faculty. Grace is the transforming uncreated energy of God which is directly responsible for our transformation and divinization.[28] By grace our fallen natures are "spiritually cleansed and inspired" by the breath, the grace, of God.

For Orthodoxy, man's proper response to the incarnation is to accept the invitation to a renewed beginning of synergy, to realign (with the constant help of grace) his own will to God's. Grace is the all-important factor in man's transformation, so all practices (*praxis*—prayer, fasting, prostrations, etc.) are viewed as means (often indispensable means) to the end of "purity of heart," a state of receptivity to the Holy Spirit (grace).[29] The noetic "unceasing prayer" of hesychastic practice is the highest form of man's attempt to let the *means* correspond to the *end*. We have seen how apophatic theology can play a role in spirituality; man's mind may be properly disposed toward the "unknowability" of God. Yet as man's spirituality blossoms with the inworking of grace, man finds that all systems of thought, indeed everything that comes from man, ultimately mean nothing in relation to God. As Dionysios said, God is beyond affirmation *and* denial. In the "simplicity" of noetic

(28) Lossky expresses this as follows: "The fruit of prayer is divine love, which is simply grace, appropriated in the depths of our being. For love, according to Diadochus, is not simply a movement of the soul; but is also an uncreated gift—a divine energy—which continually inflames the soul and unites it to God by the power of the Holy Spirit" (p. 212).

(29) Cf. St. Serafim of Sarov's particularly poignant defense of practice (*praxis*) as a "means to an end": "Prayer, fasting, watching, and all other Christian acts, however good they may be, do not alone constitute the aim of our Christian life, although they serve as the indispensable means of reaching this aim. The true aim of our Christian life, is to acquire the Holy Spirit of God." This quote is from "A Conversation of St. Seraphim of Sarov with Nicholas Motovilov concerning the Aim of the Christian Life," reprinted in volume 2 of the *Collected Works* of George P. Fedotov, *A Treasury of Russian Spirituality* (Belmont, Mass.: Nordland, 1975), p. 267. Concerning "purity of heart," see Lossky, p. 203. Regarding "receptivity," Lossky notes that "the nature of spiritual prayer in the tradition of the Christian East consists in making the heart ready for the indwelling of grace by constantly guarding its interior purity" (p. 211).

prayer, one may witness a far purer expression of man's attempt to understand (receive) Christ without accommodating him to man's own view of the world.[30] Here one gathers oneself and, with one's sinful view of the world, falls before the feet of Christ, that he might, in his purity and according to his will, "have mercy on a sinner." Christ humbly besought and received in unceasing prayer truly becomes both the *means* and the *end*.

The New Cosmos and Novus Homo. As man is transformed by the inpouring of grace, he is literally divinized,[31] he becomes the "new man." His *theosis* comes solely from participation in the divine nature (the uncreated energies of God), not from anything that resides in his own nature. Nevertheless, by the indwelling of the grace of God, man's human faculties—his intellect and body—"are spiritually cleansed and inspired."[32] With such a cleansing man finds that his fallen world, which has its source in his own fallen nature, begins to fade and be replaced by the New Heaven and the New Earth. Man's vision is transformed and, consequently, so is the world in which he dwells. With the incarnation, man may actually transform the world! This casting down of the old world and the old order (death and destruciton) is what we spoke of earlier as man's "divinely-appointed function." It is that for which "the whole creation has been groaning in travail . . ." (Rom 8:22). In and

(30) Citing St. Mark the Hermit, Lossky contends that "far from seeking ecstasy or a state of excitement, the spirit must be constantly on its guard against giving any particular image to the Godhead. . . . In freeing itself completely from all conceptualization of the godhead, 'the spirit receives into itself the characteristics of a deiform image and becomes clothed with the ineffable beauty of the likeness of the Lord' " (pp. 211-12).

(31) Some sense of this notion is found in Fr. Georges Florovsky's discussion of St. Gregory Palamas and the patristic tradition: "Man now is admitted into an intimate 'communion' with God, through Christ and by the power of the Holy Spirit. And this is much more than just a 'moral' communion, and much more than just a human perfection. Only the word *theosis* can render adequately the uniqueness of the promise and offer. . . . It is that intimate intercourse of man with God, in which the whole of human existence is, as it were, permeated by the Divine Presence." *Collected Works,* vol. 1, *Bible, Church, Tradition: An Eastern Orthodox View* (Belmont, Mass.: Nordland, 1972), p. 115.

(32) Romanides, p. 229.

through Christ (and assuredly *only* so), man may fulfill that potential to which he has been called for ages. As the Golden-Mouthed St. John hymns this potential in his Easter Homily:

O Death, where is thy sting? O Hades, where is thy victory?

Christ is risen and thou art cast down.

Christ is risen and the demons have fallen.

Christ is risen and the angels rejoice.

Christ is risen and life is made free.

Christ is risen and there is none dead in the tomb.

For Christ is raised form the dead and become the first-fruits of them that slept.

To Him be glory and dominion from all ages to all ages!

Amen.

2

History and Politics of the Byzantine Church: Some Historiographical Perspectives

by

ARCHIMANDRITE CHRYSOSTOMOS

With both some relief and deserved pride, Eastern Christians have seen, in the last three or four decades of this century, a virtual "renaissance" of interest in their traditions and beliefs. Both eastern and western writers have triumphed the great struggle of the Orthodox Church through cataclysmic political upheavals, years of domination by hostile forces, and incredible misrepresentation by western observers of her life and spirit. The present essay is in no manner designed to minimize or criticize the happy event of this rebirth. Rather, it proposes to provide some perspectives on the development of the Byzantine Church that earlier commentaries on eastern ecclesiology simply ignored.

It is not as though many of the more egregious misrepresentations of the eastern witness have not been clarified by modern writers. The issue at point is that the emergence of a new historiographical approach to the Christian East has been largely an outgrowth of the ecumenical spirit—one which sees no reason to confront the old prejudices and distortions. As a result, many western writers are more facile in, for example, the hesychastic and mystical traditions of Eastern Orthodoxy (of no small popularity in the West today) than some Orthodox writers themselves. But in areas where the ecumenical *Zeitgeist* has not yet reached, they are prone to rely on the historical literature. Here they often come to error or offer apologies for ostensible foibles in Eastern Christianity that rise more from the

"History and Politics of the Byzantine Church: Some Historiographical Perspectives" appeared in *Kleronomia* (the journal of the Patriarchal Institute for Patristic Studies) 3:2 (1976) 293-305. Reprinted by permission.

weakness of their sources than from that of the Church. Hope-fully we can encourage a view which obviates some of these latter transgressions.

Traditional considerations of Oriental Christianity have tended to treat the eastern churches as though they had no real history. Even a commentator so sympathetic as Arthur P. Stan-ley, whose lectures on eastern ecclesiastical history enjoy a century later some of the same success that greeted them at publication, fails to resist the temptation of casting that history in a substantially negative light. He bemoans the fact that Eastern Christianity has suffered from the stagnancy of the cultures in which it flourished and from an ecclesiastical system that has "produced hardly any permanent works of practical Christian benevolence." Despite these misgivings, however, Professor Stanley concedes that his study of the eastern churches led him to find "some salient scenes and epochs which beyond question touch the universal destinies of man."[1] But on the whole, such concessions are but small points of light in that immense shadow which fell over eastern ecclesiastical history from the pen of Gibbon and which darkened the Orthodox spirit for more years than one would care to recall.

If the study of eastern ecclesiastical history has suffered from the imposition of alien cultural standards, it has been even more markedly beset by misunderstanding and uncritical atten-tion. Nothing in this sense is more revealing than the random use of names to refer to the churches of the East and the fre-quency with which these various churches are wrongly grouped together where divisions, indeed, exist, or divided where unity is the fact. The churches of the East as a whole are often called the Eastern Church, as though they comprised a single entity, and the national Eastern Orthodox churches are often called by their separate appellations (e.g., Greek Church or Russian Church) and treated as though they were not part of the Orthodox unity. While the various divisions that actually constitute the

(1) Arthur P. Stanley, *Lectures on the History of the Eastern Church* (London: J. M. Dent and Co., 1961), p. 55.

Orthodox unity do not pertain to the earliest centuries of the Byzantine Church, an understanding of their interconnection is essential to an understanding of Orthodox ecclesiology in any era. This essential need becomes obvious, too, when one considers the existence, side by side, of national Orthodox churches, non-Orthodox national churches (such as the Armenian Church), and churches of the Roman *Unia* calling themselves, however incorrectly, "Orthodox."

Correctly speaking, the Eastern Church is the church of the Byzantine Empire, calling itself the Holy Apostolic Catholic Greek Orthodox Church, the Orthodox Church, the Byzantine Church, or the Greek Orthodox Church. It is the imperial church, the "Great Church" (as Stanley and others call it),[2] the eastern answer to the unifying influence of the Roman Church among the churches of Western Christendom. And because Constantinople, the "New Rome," is the historical center of its administrative functions, the Church calls itself "Roman," a term by which the Greek Orthodox under Turkish domination distinguished themselves from the Moslem population. The present-day national Orthodox churches, mainly those of Bulgaria, Georgia, Greece, Rumania, Russia, Serbia, and Syria, are in communion (despite sporadic ruptures and excepting the "Old Calendarist" and "Traditionalist" movements in the last five or six decades) with the Patriarchate of Constantinople and, though they may have their own patriarchates, maintain the historical Constantinopolitan unity of the Eastern Church. The Patriarch of Constantinople is regarded as the *primus inter pares* of the Orthodox bishops. The Church of Russia, for example, is at once Russian, Greek, Orthodox, Eastern, Byzantine, and Catholic. It is a distinguished member of a greater whole.

It is proper to speak of the remaining bodies of Eastern Christendom as the eastern churches. They include those Christians who resisted the standardizing influence of the Constantinopolitan Byzantine Church. In the theological lexicon of the early councils, they are heretical sects, usually united along

(2) Ibid., p. 64.

19

national lines. The Armenian Church is perhaps the largest of the national churches of the East having no direct contact with the Byzantine Church. It nonetheless often calls itself Orthodox and is in many ways theologically close to the Greek Church. The absence of the Armenian bishops from the Council of Chalcedon, thus not receiving its decrees, is the reason for the church's heresy in the eyes of Byzantium. The churches of Syria exist alongside the national Syrian Orthodox Church, with the latter's Patriarchate in Antioch.[3] The first of the national non-Orthodox churches, the Jacobite or Monophysite Church, is the surviving church of the monophysite heretics. The second church, founded in the fifth century, is that of the monothelite heretics, the Maronite Church. The Maronite Church was greatly influenced by the Roman crusaders of the twelfth century and has remained tied to the Roman papacy (though relations have often been strained, as in the last decade, to the point of rupture).

Another monophysite church, typically following only the first three ecumenical councils, is that of Egypt, the Coptic Church. Denying the human nature of Christ, it is today closely linked with the Jacobites of Syria. It is separated from the Eastern Orthodox Patriarch of Alexandria, yet considers itself to be the true Alexandrian church. The national church of Ethiopia, a fourth-century missionary church of the Patriarchate of Alexandria, is the most anomalous of the eastern churches. It adheres to both the Jewish and Christian days of worship. Polygamy flourishes with church sanction, and the ritualistic practices of dancing and beating drums prevail in liturgical functions.

What emerges from this cursory survey of the eastern churches is not only a more exact nomenclature for reference to the various bodies, but a picture of the ecclesiastical history

---

(3) The Antiochian Patriarchate claims to have been founded by St. Peter and, like all eastern churches save those of the Latin *Unia* and the Syrian Maronites, rejects the Petrine doctrines of the papacy. Despite this claim, however, many eastern Fathers and contemporary Orthodox theologians make effusive references to a certain "primacy of honor" due Rome. While these references stress the historical honor of the Roman Church, it should be noted that they absolutely reject any notion of a hierarchical or doctrinal primacy of the Bishop of Rome. Moreover, the Roman primacy of honor is shared by the Patriarch of Constantinople.

of the East. Such historical diversity itself belies the notion that eastern ecclesiastical history is tedious and stationary. Moreover, it serves as a warning to the casual observer, who so incautiously refers to the unity or uniformity of the eastern churches. The Coptic Alexandrian Church is in no way to be confused with the Alexandrian Orthodox Church (though they may have common origins) nor, to be sure, can the Syrian national churches (Jacobite or Maronite) be equated with the Syrian Orthodox Church. And as though these distinctions were not in themselves sufficiently complex, there is the added nomenclature by which each individual church chooses to designate itself. Particular attention should be drawn to the fact, previously cited, that the Eastern Christians in communion with the see of Constantinople frequently refer to their church as the "Church of Rome." Likewise, many Christians of the Latin *Unia* refer to themselves, as we mentioned, by the term "Orthodox," designating, for the greater part, nothing more than the origin of their liturgical rites and customs.

What we are confronting for our purposes here, then, is the Eastern Church, the Church of Constantinople, that imperial center which succeeded in guiding only one, yet the largest, of the eastern churches. The establishment of the Orthodox Church in the East began (in the sense of its external institution free from political persecution) with the pronouncements of the Emperor Constantine in the fourth century. The entire history of the Church was set by the church-state hegemony that Constantine initiated. Moreover, the Eastern Church is the church of the era of the "Great Peace," when Christians finally came to worship openly and without fear. It is a church that owes its external institution, freedom, and development to the Constantinopolitan throne. And to attempt to understand Eastern Orthodoxy separate from its role as the imperial church is to distort its image and fail at understanding its subsequent political actions.

Constantine rose to the imperial throne in 324, having ended the schism in the Roman Empire that followed the retirement of Diocletian. Hoping to avail himself of the wealth and power of the East, he removed the imperial capital from Rome and established a "New Rome" in Byzantium, which he named in honor of himself: Constantinople.[4] Long before the establishment of his imperial capital, Constantine embraced the Christian faith. This conversion took place before his occupation of Rome, when he was forced to engage in battle an enemy on the site of the Milvian Bridge. It is reported by Eusebius, his biographer, that before the battle Constantine saw the two Greek letters "XP" (from *Christos*) and the caption, "In this sign you shall conquer," written in the heavens. It is this experience which won him to the Christian faith.[5]

For the Christians in his empire Constantine reserved a place of honor and attention in the civil service and in the army. He made it legal to leave estates to the Church and insured and expanded the power of the bishops. In Constantinople he built a shrine to the Twelve Apostles, preparing for himself a tomb therein, reflective of his place in Orthodox hagiography today as St. Constantine, "Equal to the Apostles."[6] Constantine's activity vis-à-vis the Church reached its culmination in his calling together of the bishops in the important Council of Nicea (325), the first of the ecumenical councils. He not only presided over the council, but participated in some aspects of the theological discussions.

In spite of the edicts of Nicea, from the death of Constantine to the reign of the Emperor Theodosius (379), the Arian heresy raged. Though all of the emperors, with the exception of Julian the Apostate (361-363), were nominally Christians, they wav-

(4) We should note here that the title "New Rome" does not reflect, as some writers have incorrectly claimed, a transfer of power from the Roman Church to the Church of Constantinople. Rather, "New Rome" is a reference to the city of Constantine, in which the Christian Church surfaced as a free institution. Thus, from its very beginning the Eastern Church made claims to primacy and authenticity as the Church of Rome, not as the heir to the alleged primacy and authenticity of the bishopric of Rome.

(5) Some observers discount this apparition and even deny that Constantine was a Christian. One such writer argues that if Constantine ever did convert to Christianity, "it was probably not until he was on his deathbed." See Jeffrey B. Russell, *A History of Medieval Christianity: Prophecy and Order* (New York: Thomas H. Crowell, 1968), p. 28, Orthodox, of course, reject these views.

(6) This same type of honor is bestowed upon Constantine's mother, who was canonized St. Helena and is said to be the discoverer of the True Cross.

ered in their support of the anti-Arian edicts of the council. In each case the will of the emperor somewhat affected the Church. The effect of intervention by the empire in church affairs was becoming clear. It was in this atmosphere that a rift was to occur which would begin to emphasize the separate status of the Eastern Church. After the death of Constantine, the empire was once again divided. Of his three sons, Constantine II and Constans supported the Council of Nicea, while Constantius, ruler of the East, supported the Arian heresy. The pattern of East-West disagreement was being definitely established, this time between some eastern bishops (influenced by the will of the emperor) and their Arianism and the western bishops and their adherence to the dicta of the Nicean Creed. More importantly, the attempts of Athanasios, exiled from his Patriarchate in Alexandria, to form a united Orthodox front against the Arians by an alliance with Julian, the Roman pope, failed at the council of Sardica (343). The consequences were of two types: first, the eastern adherents to the Council of Nicea came to see themselves as separate "strugglers"; second, the reassertion of Orthodoxy in the East was to create a new school of saints and hierarchs that tended to focus attention away from the West.

Under Julian the Apostate, a council called at Alexandria after the return in 362 of the Patriarch Athanasios, though limited in effect, won back some Eastern Christians to the orthodoxy of Nicea. But the death of Julian ushered in another division. Again the western emperor supported Nicea and the eastern emperor the Arians. And now, after Athanasios had failed in inviting western cooperation in resistance to Arianism, the eastern bishops failed to seek such cooperation. Some of the greatest doctors of the Eastern Church surfaced in this struggle against Arianism and the eastern emperor. Notable among these are St. Basil the Great, St. Gregory of Nyssa, and St. Gregory of Nazianzen, the foremost members of the so-called Cappadocian school of theology. When the Arian heresy was at last conquered (on the death of the Emperor Valens in 378), the Eastern Church triumphed with its own heroes and warriors. The Council of Constantinople (381) in the reign of Theodosius I was an eastern council par excellence and the victory of the Church looked without question like a victory of the Eastern Church.

Unfortunately, the real object lesson of the Arian struggle has traditionally escaped historians, who have preferred to see it as a case of "caesaropapism," the rather pejorative term by which writers allude to the supposed submission of the Eastern Church to the will of emperor. As Michael Gough writes:

> . . . with a Christian emperor in Constantinople, and the Pope exercising a comparable, though different authority in the affairs of the West, the new situation showed itself, as Diehl has so picturesquely put it concerning the period around the Council of Chalcedon (451), in the "incongruity between the Oriental episcopate, docile to the will of the prince, and the unyielding and haughty intransigence of the Roman pontiffs."[7]

These attitudes, part of almost unquestioned historiographical approaches to the Eastern Church and the Byzantine state, are accurate to the extent that they recognize a certain subservience on the part of the eastern bishops to the state. But they are distorted in the sense that they do not fully explore the church-state model that prompted these circumstances in the East. Moreover, they fail to understand Orthodox ecclesiology, which allows for the domination of a vast portion of believers by heresy and yet views the Church as having remained wholly unified and without spot. Let us, then, more fairly assess the Byzantine church-state hegemony and more accurately face the object lesson of the Arian years.

We might first point out that any subservience on the part of the eastern bishops to the emperor was not unique to them and alien to the western bishops. The eventual domination of the Pope of Rome over the Latin Church bespeaks an acquiescence on the part of the western bishops not wholly dissimilar to that of the oriental episcopacy. The key to the Byzantine

(7) Michael Gough, *The Early Christians* (New York: Frederick A. Praeger, 1961), pp. 110-11.

24

behavior lies in the reception of state protection by the fourth-century Church. The faithful failed to resist the power of the state because:

> . . . they were too relieved to escape persecution; they were too eager to Christianize society by the use of political influence; and they were too accustomed to the formal attachment of the religion to the state. The idea of real religious pluralism was almost inconceivable to a religion that was convinced that it possessed the only ethical and metaphysical truth.[8]

While this arrangement was modified in the Western Church, it prevailed throughout the history of the Eastern Church.[9]

Of course, it is one thing to acknowledge the historical roots of the church-state hegemony in the early Church and quite another to explain its persistence into modern times. In most instances, historians view this persistence in the East as some amorphous corruption and stagnancy and turn with rapt attention to the development of precisely such an arrangement in the efforts of the Roman pontiff to establish ecclesiastical and secular order during the Western Middle Ages. Jeffrey Russell, viewing the Christian experience as a constant struggle between the quest for social order and the "prophetic spirit" of the monks and mystics (a view not original to him), deals with some of the more blatant prejudices of those who impugn the wisdom of the Eastern Church's willingness to opt for church-state hegemony in an effort not to jeopardize its acknowledged preoccupation with the mystical and prophetic traditions of Christianity:

> We are so used to looking at hereditary monarchy with the jaundiced eyes of eighteenth-century revolutionaries that we easily overlook its great virtues. The principle of hereditary succession restricts civil wars and succession disputes, and limits both the excessive power of

(8) Russell, *Medieval Christianity*, pp. 29-30.
(9) Note, for example, the persistence of Eastern Orthodox national churches and the establishment of a "Third Rome" in Moscow under the Tsars of Russia.

the army and excessive exercise of venality. Though the Byzantines changed dynasties, occasionally with violence, on eight major occasions, "Byzantine intrigue" was seldom as disruptive and never as frequent as that which contributed so heavily to the downfall of the old Roman Empire.[10]

Now we must move beyond the models that explain any subservience on the part of the Eastern Church to the caprice of the emperor and speak more directly of the social dynamics of the Eastern Church. If the Arian heresy points to the survival of Orthodox theology within a system seeing, from time to time, betrayal of that theology, it also stresses the nature of resistance to heresy that characterizes the Eastern Church. Certainly the Cappadocian school was not marked by a group of "docile" theologians. The resistance of its followers was so strong as to finally return the whole structure of the Church to the Nicean tradition. And this task was handled within the Church, not by the imposition of the will of a hierarch. It was handled within the dynamics of the Church as it interacted in the church-state structure.

This dynamic nature of the Eastern Church is so subtle as to be ignored by many observers. Often the Byzantine bishops are characterized by western writers as having no real concept of uniformity in the Church. The Roman pontiff is held up as an example of the kind of hierarch needed to avoid heresy and chaos, often as though such an arrangement simply never occurred to the Orthodox. In fact, Orthodox ecclesiology could never accommodate such a notion of the Church. For the East, the Church has always been present in its entirety where there is a bishop interacting with his flock and adhering to Orthodox beliefs. If a single bishop remains loyal to the Orthodox tradition (as was virtually the case with St. Mark of Ephesus in his resistance to the False Council of Florence), he alone constitutes the Church, though hundreds of other bishops, the Orthodox

(10) Jeffrey B. Russell, *Medieval Civilization* (New York: John Wiley and Sons, 1968), p. 117.

26

hierarchy, and the state may proclaim this or that tenet to be Orthodox. Tradition, as it were, acts as a dynamic force to perpetuate the Church. Where tradition exists, there the Church prospers; where it is absent, the Church, in the strictest sense, does not exist.

Thus it is that the Orthodox ecclesiological configuration allows for the Church to perpetuate itself from within, from the dynamic forces of interaction between members of the Church. It is then somehow inessential to the Church, in reviewing the Arian years, for example, that the emperor and some of the believers stood side by side in error. Believers in error are not the Church, and the Church need not be sought in an emperor or in a patriarch. In the Arian heresy the Cappadocian school more or less constituted the Church. (It should be noted, too, that in the Eastern Church all hierarchs, be they bishops or patriarchs, are of equal rank. No single hierarch represents or speaks for the Church as a whole. Its unity is always mystical and can never be measured by external conditions.)[11]

At this point we might look at some of the historiographical traditions of the Byzantine Church itself. How does it handle the problem of writing its own history, given the concept of social dynamics and ecclesiology mentioned above? Since the bishops admittedly served the state while pursuing their apostolic mission, they came to view both in an aura of divinity. The imperial mission (as in the case of Constantine) was a part of the soteriological schema, the emperor being a divinely instituted ruler. The aims of the emperors became in some ways divine. As a logical consequence of this divinization of the Church and its entire milieu, critical histories and considerations

(11) There is much confusion among contemporary writers regarding Orthodox ecclesiology. They find it difficult to understand how the unity of Orthodox churches can exist while external intercommunion does not. Again, Orthodox ecclesiology, except in the case of the ecumenical councils, does not conceive of the fulness of the Church in terms of external unity, the number of adherents, or the sanction of some given hierarch. It is tradition which gives unity (and this is a nontemporal, nonspatial unity), and to the extent that one adheres to tradition one is in union with the Church. Thus, the measure of unity in Orthodoxy between, say, a certain Russian local church and a certain Greek local church is not in their sharing of the sacraments *per se*, but in the extent to which each adheres to tradition; if there is full adherence, there is full unity.

of Orthodoxy have been largely absent in the East. The role of imperial influence in the Church is minimized, the claim being repeatedly made that, while the emperor is divinely instituted, it is the Church which imparts this divinity. Moreover, it is often added that church furnishings, architecture, and customs are all divinely instituted. Any casual similarity between the Church and the empire, it is asserted, is the result of the adaptation, on account of divine guidance, of Church customs and practices by the empire.

It is seldom that western writers confront Orthodox historiography. When they do, they cast it off as sheer nonsense. Even contemporary Orthodox commentators find it difficult to justify the Church's historical self-concept. Protopresbyter Alexander Schmemann, for example, writes in his *Introduction to Liturgical Theology* that, "Orthodox writers are usually inclined to 'absolutize' the history of worship, to consider the whole of it as divinely established and Providential."[12] These critical overviews, however, miss an important argument, which even tradtional Orthodox writers seldom articulate. Another protopresbyter, however, states it quite plainly in reference to liturgical practices in the Orthodox Church:

> The present rule of Divine Services was already contained in the idea of the Divine Services of the first Christians in the same way that in the seed of a plant are already contained the forms of the plant's future growth up to the moment when it begins to bear mature fruits, or in the way that in the embryonic organism of a living creature its future form is already revealed. To the foreign eye, to the non-Orthodox West, the fact that our rule has taken a static form is presented as a petrification, a fossilization; but for us this represents the finality of the form of growth, the attainment of the possible fullness and finality; and such finality of the form of development we observe also in Eastern Church iconography, in church architecture, in the interior ap-

(12) Alexander Schmemann, *Introduction to Liturgical Theology* (London: Faith Press, 1966), p. 72.

28

pearance of the best churches, in the traditional melodies of church singing.[13]

There is, then, a sense of finality among the Orthodox, a tendency to see past history as divine and to be content with the "fulness" of the Christian experience at present. Such attitudes at once discourage the cruder forms of eschatological emphasis and make the practice of historical investigation somewhat ludicrous. It is ridiculous to look at the past in an attempt to modify the present, if one views the present as the "finality of growth" of historical processes. These dispositions in Eastern Orthodox scholarship have been internally rewarding and externally disastrous. Internally, staunch adherence to tradition has afforded the various Orthodox bodies a unity which is in no manner guaranteed by a structural hierarchy or a central ecclesiastical head. In addition, the pervasive divinity implicit in the Orthodox ecclesiastical self-image is its very raison d'être. It is the witness of divinity in the world, the "burning bush."[14] As Berdyaev expressed it, the Orthodox Church is the church which feels it comes closest to the prophetic spirit of the Christian Church of St. John's vision.[15] Externally, the Church has never investigated, or at least never widely promulgated, its historical uniqueness. As result, its history has been misrepresented, linked with that of Roman Catholicism or the eastern churches in general, or simply ignored.[16]

At this point we seem to have come to a final statement regarding history and politics in the early Byzantine Church. In fact, we have reached that historical point, following the conquest over Arianism, when the Byzantine Empire and Church began to flower. But the historical perspectives gained

(13) Michael Pomazansky, "The Liturgical Theology of Fr. A. Schmemann," *Orthodox Word* (November-December 1970), n.p.

(14) See this metaphor in Ernst Benz, *The Eastern Orthodox Church: Its Thought and Life,* tr. Richard and Clara Winston (Garden City, N.Y.: Anchor Books, 1963), p. 217.

(15) Nicholas Berdyaev, *The Divine and the Human* (London: G. Bles, 1949), pp. 183-94.

(16) This habit of linking the development of the Eastern Church with that of the Western (so-called parallelism) can be observed in almost every aspect of the study of Eastern Orthodoxy up to the last several decades.

from these seminal years are pertinent to any subsequent consideration of the history of the Eastern Church. It is the very same ecclesiology that marks the Arian years which later really adequately explains the emergence of the Church from the iconoclastic controversy and her survival *as* the Eastern Church after the attempts at union in the fifteenth century. And a clear picture of the East-West schism in the earliest years of Christendom serves to dispel the naive notion that, in one dramatic event, the Church separated in 1054 and a separate eastern witness emerged. The Orthodox witness was, from the earliest years, a separate and unique one. It was a distinct voice among the many divergent voices of the East and one which was eventually to echo the words of apostolicity as the Christian East came to view it.

Finally, we cannot underestimate the role of Orthodox historiography itself in the unfortunate promulgation of misrepresentations of the Eastern Church. First, there is the critical question of self-presentation, which we have characterized as foreign to the Orthodox worldview. Eastern ecclesiastical historians have tended to regard the Church as an institution transcendent of its own history, finding it unnecessary, therefore, to explain her historical road even from their own perspectives. Second, as a result of this inimical view toward historical criticism, critical commentaries fell into the hands of those less versed in and sympathetic to the Byzantine way. Combined with a mystical cosmology, in which the Church came to fill the role of an agent in the divinization of the world and the faithful, these consequences have served to dim the light of the eastern witness and to deny to Christians a separate and unique, if not the true, model of Christian experience.[17]

(17) One cannot overestimate the unique cosmological theology of the Eastern Church, in which the Athanasian aphorism "Christ became man so that man might become divine" is taken quite literally and seriously. The Orthodox Church, particularly in her Palamite theology, stresses the possibility of man to participate, at least to a limited extent, in the joys of the *parousia* now, on earth. The Church offers a "foretaste" of that "other world," once again lifting her out of historical reality. For Christians of the Orthodox tradition, just as the Paschal experience has a significance akin to the experience of the heavenly joys, so the Church offers in her divine services nonhistorical, "other-worldly" liturgical glimpses of Christian bliss. This comes to be her central purpose and primary goal.

3

A Comparative Treatment of Scripture and Tradition in the Orthodox East and the Catholic and Protestant West

by

Hieromonk Auxentios and Archimandrite Chrysostomos

The canon, as it were, of Orthodox theology is the patristic witness, the *consensus patrum*. So it is that the Eastern Church turns to the writings of the Fathers in order to formulate her understanding of the nexus between Scripture and tradition. We have elsewhere detailed some of the early patristic writings and their contribution to that formulation.[1] However, to describe the Eastern Church's view of Scripture and tradition and its patristic roots is not in itself an adequate accomplishment. It would be fruitless to try to present the uniquely Orthodox vision of Scripture and tradition without setting against it the Roman Catholic and Protestant views on the matter. Moreover, without the perspective gained by a comparative consideration, a statement of the Orthodox position on traditional and scriptural authority is fraught with danger. Much of contemporary Orthodox theology is little more than an adaptation of western theological perspectives, resulting in an obfuscation of the bona fide Orthodox stance. To declare the inadequacy of such adaptational theology requires some comprehension of the assumptions from which the theology is drawn. Hence, a comparative context is indispensable.

"A Comparative Treatment of Scripture and Tradition in the Orthodox East and the Catholic and Protestant West" is in press in *Diakonia* (the journal of the John XXIII Center for Eastern Christian Studies, Fordham University), to appear in 1981. Printed by permission.

The authors would like to express their gratitude to Dr. Horton Davies, Putnam Professor of Religion at Princeton University, for his critical review of manuscripts from which portions of this essay were drawn.

(1) M. G. Chapman and Abbot Chrysostomos, "Scripture and Tradition in the Orthodox Church: The Early Church Witness," *Diakonia* 14:3 (1979) 213-223.

31

It should be noted at this juncture that our purpose in following a comparative course is not to develop in detail the western theological positions on scriptural and traditional authority. We wish only to identify the general perspectives from which Protestant and Roman Catholic positions are formulated, again so that we might better identify the Orthodox position as it stands out against the western view. The sundry positions that can be drawn from those perspectives and that represent the range of positions in western theology cannot receive our attention here. We simply acknowledge them and admit the limitations of our present course of investigation.

The Protestant View

Without doubt, to speak of a "Protestant position" on any subject is imprecise. Protestantism encompassses traditions too many and too diverse to confess of any single characterization. It is, then, likewise difficult to arrive at an accurate statement regarding Protestant perspectives on Scripture and tradition as sources of authority in the Church. The best that we can do in this dilemma is to restrict our consideration principally to the two most historically salient reformed movements, those of Luther and Calvin. At the very least, their utterances on Scripture and tradition have made Luther and Calvin important sources of doctrine in the contemporary formulation of Lutheran and Calvinist stands on the subject. And modern-day Lutheran and Calvinist bodies constitute, no doubt, the greater part of Protestantism today. A cursory survey cannot, of course, account for the large variance in opinions even in these denominational circles; but it can hopefully provide the perspectives from which the many opinions arise. These perspectives, albeit limited in the sense we have mentioned, will afford some comparative scope.

The Lutheran Outlook. As a point of historical interest, we might note that Luther's attitude toward scriptural and traditional authority was not one that developed spontaneously. Indeed, it developed over a number of years. The so-called "Reformation principle *sola scriptura"* [Scripture alone], as one writer calls it, "was not expressed in its full form until 1520."[2] While Luther's earliest theological works, his lectures on the Psalms (1513-1515), show a strong dependence on the Scriptures, they in no sense impugn ecclesiastical tradition. In fact, his hermeneutical and exegetical styles were typical of the Middle Ages. It was not until later that the authority of Scripture entirely supplanted that of tradition. As F. J. Taylor describes this gradual development in Luther's position:

> The failure of the papacy to respond to his appeal drew Luther by successive stages to a position from which he challenged, on the basis of Scripture alone, the divine institution and authority of the papal office. His own experience had taught him that God spoke directly, through His written word, to the heart of the believer and from his experience he proceeded to erect a new criterion of authority. The very greatness of his religious genius thus led him both to disallow contemporary forms of ecclesiastical authority and to a certain brusque impatience with tradition.[3]

The final form of Luther's attitude toward Scripture and authority is fairly well represented in his treatise on the ministry, addressed to the "Illustrious Senate and People of Prague."[4] Speaking of priestly tonsure and anointing, Luther dismisses the practices as "superstition," going on to endorse only those practices which are purely scriptural:

> We are interested in the pure and true course, prescribed in holy Scripture, and are little concerned about usage or what the fathers have said or done in this matter. We have already sufficiently made clear that herein we neither ought, should, nor would be bound by human tra-

(2) Berndt Moeller, "Scripture, Tradition, and Sacrament in the Middle Ages and in Luther," in F. F. Bruce and E. G. Rupp, eds., *Holy Book and Holy Tradition* (Manchester, 1968), p. 130.

(3) F. J. Taylor, "Scripture and Tradition in the Anglican Reformation," in F. W. Dillistone et al., *Scripture and Tradition* (London, 1955), pp. 55f.

(4) Martin Luther, "Concerning the Ministry," in Helmut T. Lehmann, ed., *Luther's Works*, vol. 40 (Philadelphia, 1958), p. 7.

ditions, however sacred and highly regarded. . . .[5]
In a later passage, Luther makes it quite clear that only Scripture, and not traditions "approved only by the use of centuries and the multitudes,"[6] can suffice as a basis for authority in the Church. He argues that even when an "innovation" is "most recent, . . . if the Word of God here enlightens and commands us, and the need of souls compels it, then the novelty of the thing ought not at all to affect us, but the majesty of the Word."[7]

We would be remiss were we to leave our discussion of Luther as such seeming to suggest that it is *in toto* the perspective from which contemporary Lutheran theology might draw. In fact, Luther does not, in his arguments, wholly abjure tradition. In one place he speaks sympathetically of an ancient custom (again, sacerdotal tonsure and anointing) as having been "abolished and destroyed by the contrary examples and pestilential teachings of the papists."[8] Luther's concern seems to be more with the abuse of tradition than with its insufficiency as a source of authority. Moreover, as one authority has quite correctly asserted, the great Lutheran apologist Melanchthon presents a view of tradition that may emerge from the Lutheran posture as purged from the somewhat polemical pen of Luther.[9] Melanchthon, in fact, argues that the early Fathers were saintly men and that, since they were so near in time to Christ and the Apostles, their writings could be assumed to faithfully express the witness of Scripture. Though we should keep in mind this broader outlook on tradition within Lutheran theology, we should not mistake it for a principle that mediates the authority of "Scripture alone," which remains *à outrance* the Lutheran perspective.

The Calvinist Outlook. In the writings of Calvin we find a clear repudiation of the authority of ecclesiastical tradition and

(5) Ibid.
(6) Ibid., pp. 38f.
(7) Ibid., p. 39.
(8) Ibid.
(9) Consult P. Lengsfeld, *Überlieferung: Tradition und Schrift in der Evangelischen und Katholischen Theologie der Gegenwart* (Paderborn, 1960), pp. 150-55.

an equally evident approbation of the absolute ascendancy of scriptural authority. In his tract, "On the Necessity of Reforming the Church," Calvin holds that church traditions, such as abstaining from meat on Friday and priestly celibacy, are mere human inventions and even in discord with scriptural law:

> For where is the incomparable majesty of God, after mortal man has been exalted to such a height that his laws take precedence of God's eternal decrees? I omit that an apostle describes the prohibitions of meats and of marriage as a doctrine of devils, (I Tim. 4:1-3). That is surely bad enough; but the crowning impiety is to set man in a higher rank than God.[10]

He affirms, further, in another essay that "all true religion has been perverted by keeping the commandments of men," and admonishes that by "warnings from common experience, . . . we are the more confined in not passing the limits of Scripture."[11]

Calvin's rejection of tradition is, in a sense, made on hermeneutic grounds. Writing on the Council of Trent, he addresses some rather terse words to the council members—"those degenerate and bastard sons of the Roman See, *i.e.*, the great harlot. . . ."[12] He takes umbrage with the Tridentine claim that Scripture must be interpreted by the "holy mother Church" on the grounds that any "gross old wife's dream" might be given credence on the basis of the Church's interpretive authority.[13] And, while he admits that some traditions may well be of apostolic origin, he maintains that others are "unworthy" of that admission.[14] Thus, accedence to the authority of tradition potentially leads to the same abuses engendered by a recognition of the interpretive authority of the Church as such. Furthermore, since the Church's interpretive authority is often drawn from

(10) John Calvin, "The Necessity of Reforming the Church," in T. F. Torrance, ed., *Tracts and Treatises in Defense of the Reformed Faith*, tr. Henry Beveridge, vol. 1 (Grand Rapids: Eerdmans, 1958), p. 177.

(11) See Calvin's essay "Confession of Faith in Name of the Reformed Churches of France," in ibid., 2:148.

(12) John Calvin, "Acts of the Council of Trent, With the Antidote," ibid., 3:67.

(13) Ibid., p. 66.

(14) Ibid., p. 69.

the witness of tradition, Calvin implicitly denies the very authority of tradition in his disavowal of the interpretive authority of the Church.

Against the interpretive authority of the Church and the authority of tradition Calvin pits the singular witness of Scripture. He alleges that the truth of Scripture is evident in Scripture itself and that the hermeneutic usefulness of church tradition (or church authority in general) is superseded by the Word of God as its right meaning is revealed by the Holy Spirit:

> He [Calvin] understood that the divine origin and character of Scripture rested not upon the authoritative certificate of an ecclesiastical hierarchy, but upon the activity of the Holy Spirit who alone could assure the believer that these particular writings were none other than the Word of God. Scripture was thus declared to be not merely the carefully preserved divine archives, to be consulted on occasion, in order to discover what God had once spoken to the prophets and apostles, but also an immediate utterance of the spirit.[15]

For Calvin the Holy Spirit is in Scripture, the Word of God, and in the individual Christian, who, by the Spirit's activity, can recognize the valid interpretation of Scripture and rest upon its singular authority and sufficiency for salvation.

Eastern Orthodoxy and the Protestant View. We must here note that the Orthodox perspective on scriptural and traditional authority is distinguished by the fact that the early Church envisioned Scripture and tradition in an authoritative unity. Such a perspective is divergent with the two Protestant perspectives we have recounted. For one thing, because "the separation of the Fathers [tradition] from the rest of the life of the church is alien to Orthodox theology," both *"Sola Scriptura . . .* [and] *. . .Sola Tradito* have no place in the scheme of Orthodox theology."[16] Moreover, since the separa-

---

(15) Taylor, p. 56. See also Calvin's own words on the Holy Spirit and Scripture in H. T. Kerr, ed., *A Compend of the Institutes of the Christian Religion* (Philadelphia, 1939), p. 18.

(16) G. S. Bebis, "The Concept of Tradition in the Fathers of the Church," *Greek Orthodox Theological Review* 15:1 (1970) 26 and 27.

tion of Scripture and tradition is inconceivable to the East, the very notion of Scripture encountered in the Lutheran and Calvinist formulations is foreign to the Orthodox theological outlook.

To Luther's concept of Scripture as speaking to the heart of man directly the East has no response. Similarly, the Orthodox Church cannot be held answerable to Calvin's proposition that the Holy Spirit speaks through the Scriptures. For Eastern Orthodoxy, the Fathers, tradition, the Scriptures, indeed the Church herself are, in perfect unity, the sources of truth. One element cannot be separated from the other, nor can one element assume unique authority apart from and over and above its interaction with, and as a part of, the other elements. Orthodox ecclesiology, then, can never admit of the action of the Holy Spirit being concentrated or exclusively present in one single aspect of the Church. The Bible and tradition or church authority, as Professor Nissiotis has asserted, are in absolute unity.[17] A church outside this unity is not the Orthodox Church; Scripture outside this unity is not Scripture as the Orthodox Church receives it. Indeed, *sola scriptura,* under any circumstances whatever, is an unthinkable formula for the Eastern Church.

The Roman Catholic View

The Roman Catholic view on Scripture and tradition was formally set forth in the sixteenth century. The Council of Trent, summarizing their reception in the Church, acknowledges the twofold authority of Scripture and tradition:

> Saving truths and rules of conduct . . . are contained in the written books and in unwritten traditions, which . . . have come down to us, transmitted as it were from hand to hand. . . . Following, then the examples of the orthodox Fathers, it receives and venerates with a feeling of piety and reverence all the books of the Old and New Testaments, since one God is the

(17) N. A. Nissiotis, "The Unity of Scripture and Tradition: An Eastern Orthodox Contribution to the Prolegomena of Hermeneutics," *Greek Orthodox Theological Review* 11:2 (1966) 188-89.

author of both; also the traditions, whether they relate
to faith or to morals, as having been dictated either
orally by Christ or by the Holy Ghost, and preserved
in the Catholic Church in unbroken succession.[18]

Fr. Yves Congar affirms, in his consideration of Scripture and
tradition in the contemporary Roman Church, that the expression
of God's will "includes both tradition and Scripture."[19] He
further points out that Christian truth is communicated by tradition, "that method of communication . . . most essential to
the Church," and that if the Scriptures were unknown to us,
"tradition alone would suffice."[20] Fr. Congar goes on to make
a functional distinction between Scripture and tradition. He compares the role of Scripture in the Church with ". . . that played
in the preservation of ancient monuments by what is called a
witness: *testis, tertius*, . . . [*an*] element which remains fixed
and serves to measure the development of the . . . [other ele-
ments]."[21] By the same token, it is ecclesiastical tradition, Congar alleges, that interprets Scripture. And while "Tradition
envelops and transcends Scripture," the two are integrally connected.[22]

One should not suppose that Scripture and tradition in the
Roman Catholic view constitute, in their unity, the actual authority of the Church. We have some inkling of what is meant
by church authority in Augustine's famous proclamation that,
"For my part, I should not believe the gospel except as moved
by the *authority* [emphasis ours] of the Catholic Church."[23] He
appeals not to a *consensus patrum* or to holy tradition, but to

(18) From the fourth session of the council. See H. J. Schroeder, tr. and ed., *Canons
and Decrees of the Council of Trent* (St. Louis, 1941), p. 17.

(19) Yves Congar, *The Meaning of Tradition*, tr. A. N. Woodrow, (New York:
Hawthorne Books, 1964), p. 23.

(20) Ibid.

(21) Ibid., p. 95.

(22) Ibid.

(23) Augustine, "Against the Epistle of Manichaeus Called Fundamental," in P.
Schaff and H. Wace, eds., *A Select Library of Nicene and Post-Nicene Fathers*, second
series, vol. 4 (New York, 1894), p. 131.

the Church's "authority" (using the Latin, *auctoritas*).[24] He seems to be appealing to a more general authority. This general authority has come to be known in the Roman Catholic Church as the *magisterium,* the teaching authority of the Church. It is this church authority by which church matters are decided. Just as tradition "envelops" Scripture, so the *magisterium* encompasses both Scripture and tradition, becoming the final criterion of truth with "reference to Scripture and tradition."[25]

We must, then, understand Scripture and tradition as two channels of authority that feed into the greater *magisterium* of the Church. Their relationship is rightly understood only in the light of the teaching authority of the Church. And the teaching authority of the Church can be correctly apprehended only as one understands the papacy. Following Cardinal Newman's (d. 1890) doctrine of tradition, Günter Biemer argues that ". . . no other authority exists except that of the infallible *magisterium.* It is only by this gift of infallibility in the church that the transmission of teaching from generation to generation, by means of tradition, can be ultimately justified."[26] Noting that Cardinal Newman, in his earlier writings, distinguished between the concepts of papal infallibility and the infallibility of the Church, Biemer maintains that the two concepts are in fact "essentially linked" and that "the infallibility of the pope signals the place where the infallibility of the Church is embodied."[27]

The authority of the Church as it is manifested in the infallibility of the pope introduces a perspective on Scripture and tradition that is uniquely Roman Catholic. The papacy comes to represent the virtual authority of Scripture and tradition themselves. Accordingly, Pius IX, in a letter to the Archbishop of Cologne (dated October 28, 1870), contends that the definition of a dogma by the pope is in itself sufficient evidence for every-

(24) PG 42-43: 176.
(25) Congar, p. 95.
(26) Günter Biemer, *Newman on Tradition,* tr. Kevin Smyth (London: Burns and Oates, 1967), p. 106.
(27) Ibid.

thing that is founded in Scripture and tradition.[28] In short, the very authority of the papacy witnesses to the truth of Scripture and tradition. The *magisterium* of the papacy, in fact, is beyond the witness of the *consensus patrum* (tradition as we have partly defined it) and the limits of Scripture; as Pope Pius IX declared so resoundingly, "La tradizione son' io" ["I am tradition"]. The papacy becomes a tradition above and beyond the word as we have understood it, transcending the Tridentine unity of Scripture and tradition and speaking of a greater authority, the supreme *magisterium*.

It would be wrong to leave our consideration of the Roman Catholic view of Scripture and tradition as it now stands. We have suggested that the Roman perspective is comprised of four elements: firstly, the Tridentine declaration of the unity of Scripture and tradition; secondly, the distinction between Scripture and tradition on a functional level, in which tradition gains ascendancy over Scripture; thirdly, the authority of the *magisterium* as it rises above the authority of Scripture and tradition; and lastly, the embodiment of the *magisterium* in the papacy. The perspective which these four elements form, however, is often disputed in contemporary Roman Catholic thought. Even the Second Vatican Council (by a two-thirds majority vote on November 20, 1962), for example, failed to adopt the Tridentine formula of Scripture and tradition as "two sources of revelation."[29] J. R. Geiselmann of Tübingen University, in addition, has recently contended that tradition does not, in the final analysis, encompass Scripture, but that all tradition itself has at least an implicit scriptural basis.[30] And one need not belabor, finally, the popular movements against papal infallibility (and the concomitant appeal to conciliar or episcopal authority) which plague the modern Roman Church. Notwithstanding these latter re-

(28) A portion of this letter is quoted in Paul Tschackert, *Evangelische Polemik Gegen die Römische Kirche* (Gotha, 1855), p. 407, n. 16.

(29) Reference to the council's vote is found in J. A. Fichtner's article on "Tradition," in the *New Catholic Encyclopedia*, vol. 14 (New York: McGraw-Hill, 1967), pp. 225-28.

(30) See the full development of this argument in J. R. Geiselmann, *Die Heilige Schrift und die Tradition* (Freiburg, 1961).

joinders, however, the Roman Catholic perspective as we have presented it still prevails as the consensus attitude in the Church. Thus it is that Fr. Congar's notion of tradition, as we have presented it above, is pretty much the standard Catholic scholarly perspective today.

Eastern Orthodoxy and the Roman Catholic View. We should now unequivocally say that for the Eastern Orthodox Scripture and tradition, as they exist in a particular pneumatic unity, cannot be opposed to or subsumed by a greater notion of church authority, as in the Roman Catholic conceptualization of the *magisterium.* The spirit of the East has always been, as one authority observes, "more speculative, mystical and passive," while that of the West has been "active, pragmatic, legal, [and] political."[31] As a consequence, it is unthinkable in the East to separate the elements of church authority (as we pointed out in our discussion of Orthodox objections to the Protestant dichotomization of Scripture and tradition into separate entities),[32] just as it is to conceive of an ultimate authority above Scripture and tradition in any but a wholly mystical fashion. A concept of authority that could engender a slogan such as "the Church precedes the Bible,"[33] or envision a personal *magisterium,* is simply too analogous to a legalistic arrangement to commend itself to the Eastern Church.

Therefore, we must be careful not to appropriate for the Eastern Church a supposed accord with the Roman Catholic Church on Scripture and tradition, as encyclopedic treatments are wont to do. To assume, because the eastern and western churches inherited from the early Church a common belief in Scripture and tradition as joint sources of authority, that they received that belief in the same manner is naive. With such assumptions, Professor González-Alexopoulos maintains, "a vague and often weakly articulated concept of parallel devel-

---

(31) J. L. Hromádka, "Eastern Orthodoxy," in E. J. Jurji, ed., *The Great Religions of the Modern World* (Princeton: Princeton University Press, 1946), p. 288.

(32) We might interject here, in support of our contention, Archimandrite Kallistos Ware's injunction that "one should not separate Scripture and Tradition." See his book *The Orthodox Church* (Baltimore: Penguin Books, 1963), p. 207.

(33) Nissiotis, p. 190.

opment persists, seemingly uncompromised by its own insufficiency."[34] Parallelism, to be sure, obscures cases of divergent development and equally masks the subtle distinctions that make up the divergencies in Eastern Orthodox and Roman Catholic theological traditions.

We need simply point to the development of the papal *magisterium* as a case of divergent development between the eastern and western churches. The unity of Scripture and tradition in Orthodoxy developed as a statement of the two elements as they witnessed and embodied the mystical authority of the Church. In Roman Catholicism, the unity of Scripture and tradition developed hand in hand with the power of the papacy. Scripture and tradition were thus changed, in the eyes of the Eastern Church, in that they no longer embodied ecclesiastical authority, but grew to be elements juxtaposed to (if not embodied by) that authority. The unity of Scripture and tradition came to serve papal doctrine, conceived as a political authority, an "idea of jurisdictional supremacy," as one author writes.[35] In the East, such authority is unknown, except in an external sense.[36] But true authority, the action of the Holy Spirit as evidenced in the unified revelation of Scripture and tradition, is wholly mystical: "Not even Christ should be understood and looked upon as an authority to which the Church is subordinated."[37] The primary gravamina of the Orthodox against the Roman Catholic view of the unity of Scripture and tradition are a matter of the spirit in which that unity reaches the Roman see. There are, in the very strictest sense, no parallels between the perspectives of the two churches; for, the latter receives Scripture in a legalistically formulated interconnection, the former in an ineffably mystical unity.

(34) A. E. J. González-Alexopoulos, "The Byzantine Imperial Paradigm and Eastern Liturgical Vesture," *Greek Orthodox Theological Review* 17:2 (1972) 255.

(35) Ernst Benz, *The Eastern Orthodox Church: Its Thought and Life,* tr. Richard and Clara Winston (Garden City, N.Y.: Anchor Books, 1963), p. 45.

(36) Thus it is that the Eastern Orthodox Church can make effusive concessions to a primacy of honor due Rome (the same primacy of honor also owed Constantinople) and yet never conceive of any spiritual primacy accruing to that external condition.

(37) Hromádka, p. 291. Professor Hromádka goes on to note that "the Church *is* the Incarnate Christ, His life is her life" (p. 291).

4

Dom David Knowles on Hesychasm: A Palamite Rejoinder

by

HIEROMONK AUXENTIOS

It has been some years now since Dom David Knowles published his short treatise *Christian Monasticism*. While the book has met with enthusiastic interest in some quarters, it seems that there are serious objections, on the part of Eastern Orthodox writers, to Dom Knowles' treatment of the monastic tradition of the Christian East. Yet, no decisive and clear exposition of Orthodox qualifications to that treatment has been rendered. The present essay, in a somewhat apologetic tone, proposes to make such qualifications.

Knowles makes the following observation in his chapter "Byzantine Monasticism":

> In the later Greek empire true evangelical mysticism was obscured by theologians who attempted to express all experience in terms of dogma, law and logic, and enthusiasts and spiritual directors who taught that the mystical experience could be obtained by merely human efforts, whether in silencing the faculties or in some "open sesame" of continual prayer or mental effort.[1]

Apparently inexplicably setting aside the immense esteem Eastern Orthodox have always held for the sacred institution of monasticism—as the preserver of true Christian spirituality ("true evangelical mysticism")—Knowles continues to speak about what he feels is only a facet of the "controversy":

> In Byzantine monachism, the controversy . . . concerned the school of spirituality known as hesychasm. . . . The revival of interest in mystical prayer . . . drew inspi-

"Dom David Knowles on Hesychasm: A Palamite Rejoinder" appeared in *Kleronomia* 8:1 (1976) 100-106. Reprinted by permission.

(1) David Knowles, *Christian Monasticism* (New York: World University Library, 1969), p. 133.

ration from the traditional and orthodox spirituality of [Saint] Symeon [949-1022; a member of the "later Greek empire"], but taught a quasi-physical technique of a fixed gaze, regulated breathing and the repetition of the "Jesus prayer" as a means of attaining receptive, contemplative silence.[2]

Mentioning the objections of the monk Barlaam to these apparently innovative "techniques" (which seem to correspond to the previously referenced "obscurities" introduced by the "enthusiasts and spiritual directors"), Dom Knowles goes on to introduce Barlaam's opponent and the presumably futile efforts of that opponent to defend the hesychasts:

He [Barlaam] was countered by a hesychast monk and theologian, [Saint] Gregory Palamas [1296-1359], but the latter's teaching on the mystic's vision of God was in turn denounced as unorthodox, as bringing the unknowable God within the range of human (though admittedly God-aided) cognition.[3]

Knowles' scholarship is indeed wanting in his treatment of the hesychastic controversy. His statements on the subject are surprisingly lacking in critical accuracy. First of all, the whole of St. Gregory Palamas' teachings have been regarded as Orthodox since the Council of 1351 at Blacherne (within St. Gregory's own lifetime).[4] This and the fact that Palamas was proclaimed a saint at the Council of Constantinople (1368) are points which Dom Knowles sees fit to overlook, leaving the uninitiated reader with the rather unfortunate impression that initial reactions to St. Gregory's teachings as "unorthodox" prevailed uncorrected in the Eastern Church.[5]

Secondly, Knowles accuses the Orthodox Church in the "later Greek empire" of having "obscured" what he calls "true evangelical mysticism," of having introduced quasi-physical

(2) Ibid.
(3) Ibid.
(4) George G. Papademetriou, *Introduction to St. Gregory Palamas* (New York: Philosophical Library, 1973), pp. 25-26.
(5) Ibid., pp. 70-71.

techniques that were not found in traditional and orthodox spirituality. On a scholarly level, Knowles' accusation of innovations ("obscurities") borders on error. The textual evidence for historical precedents of these "quasi-physical" techniques, even in the days of "true evangelical mysticism," is at least inconclusive, if not preponderantly in support of the Eastern Orthodox. And this is without taking into account either the oral traditions that had passed unrecorded from spiritual father to spiritual son, or the spiritual ("noetic") insight of men like St. Gregory (whom the Church views as having entered into deification during his earthly existence) in these ostensibly inconclusive texts.

Knowles might have pointed out that St. Gregory Palamas (and Orthodoxy with him) was, on one front, making precisely a historical argument against the attackers of these quasi-physical techniques. St. Gregory quotes liberally from the Scriptures (with twenty-nine citations in his nine-page apology, "On the Blessed Hesychasts"), and finds precedence for his words in several of the ancient Fathers. Of St. Symeon the New Theologian (a member of the "later Greek empire" whom Knowles paradoxically found to be of "traditional and orthodox spirituality"), St. Gregory says that "to call his writings writings of life would not be sinning against truth."[6] In short, in finding support in the teachings of both the ancient Fathers and those "who have lived shortly before us," St. Gregory is making an argument for the hesychasts that is precisely *against* innovation.

> But we have talked personally with some of these saints and had them as our teachers. How can we presume to disregard these men, taught by grace and experience, and give way to those who dare to teach by means of an intricate and artful tangle of words, inspired by arrogance?[7]

It seems that Knowles has confused true Orthodoxy in the "later Greek empire" with men like Barlaam the Calabrian

(6) E. Kadloubovsky and G. E. H. Palmer, trs., *Early Fathers from the Philokalia* (London: Faber and Faber, 1969), p. 408.

(7) Ibid., p. 409.

(i.e., her opponents), who taught by an "intricate and artful tangle of words," or, as Knowles might have expressed it had he known whom to accuse, "who attempted to express all experience in terms of dogma, law and logic."

Thirdly, Knowles' labeling of hesychastic practice as a "quasi-physical" technique is unnecessarily polemic, pejorative, and misleading. And if his earlier reference—to the "enthusiasts and spiritual directors who taught that the mystical experience could be obtained by merely human efforts, whether in silencing the faculties or in some 'open sesame' of continual prayer or mental effort"—was directed at the hesychasts, his treatment merits the categorization of calumny. To suggest that Orthodox, Christians par excellence as they saw it, thought that they could bring themselves into "Divine Communion" merely by human efforts is tantamount to an accusation of gross heresy and represents less-than-pristine scholarship. Hesychastic practice represents the height of what Orthodoxy calls "synergy," the cooperation of man, in his will and his efforts, with the divine will. Both the human and the divine actions are seen as necessary, although (of course) the divine workings take precedence in everything (time, efficacy, purity, etc.).

For St. Gregory, *all* of the spiritual practices of hesychasm (which may have physical components—thus Knowles' misnomer, "quasi-physical techniques") are viewed simply as a means to an end. That "end" is a state of receptivity ("purity of heart") to the working of the divine will in man, to grace. Hence, hesychastic practice, in either its mental or spiritual components, simply *allows* the working of the divine will in men—it does not necessitate it. Prayer, fasting, prostrations, and all other spiritual practices are the human components of synergy, the divine component being completely beyond man's control (though the Fathers—indeed, the Scriptures—express confidence in the steadfastness of the divine will):

He who purifies his body by self-mastery, who by love makes anger and lust an occasion for virtue, and who teaches the mind, cleansed by prayer, to stand before

God, will receive and see in himself the grace promised
to the pure in heart.[8]

If there seems to be confusion between the divine and human
actions in effecting the divine union (as in, "it is intense prayer
by its holy action that accomplishes the soaring of man to God
and union with Him"),[9] this is simply because God, in his
Grace, is seen as already dwelling within man and working
through him.

If, according to the Apostle, "God hath sent forth the
spirit of His son into your hearts, crying, Abba, Father"
(Gal. 4:6), how can we pray with this spirit, if not with
our hearts?[10]

Finally, Knowles, in his far-from-respectful choice of
words, may be implying that there is something nonevangelical
or even un-Christian in the physical components of hesychastic
practice. If so, he is dealing with something at the heart of
Orthodox dogma, theology, and spirituality, not simply the
misguided experiments of a few "enthusiasts and spiritual directors."

St. Gregory Palamas' apology "On the Blessed Hesychasts"
is a defense of the hesychastic (Orthodox) view that the mind
should be kept within the body in its search for union with God.
His defense is not lacking in scriptural (historical and spiritual)
verification:

Brother! Do you not hear the Apostle saying that "your
body is the temple of the Holy Ghost, which is in you"
(2 Cor. 6:19), and again, that "ye are the temple of
God" (1 Cor. 3:16), as God also says, "I will dwell
in them and walk in them; and I will be their God"
(2 Cor. 6:16)? Who, then, possessing a mind, will deem
it unseemly to introduce his mind into that which has
been granted the honour of being the dwelling of God?[11]

(8) Ibid., p. 403.
(9) Ibid., p. 409.
(10) Ibid., p. 404.
(11) Ibid., pp. 401-2.

These scriptural passages were upheld precisely because the hesychasts knew, from their own experience, what the consequences of ecstatic, extracorporal experience were. Father Romanides, writing on the Palamite controversy, notes that:

> It is the noetic faculty [the mind, for our purposes] as an energy of the soul which must be circumscribed within the body and thus guarded against the wanderings of contemplation, of being occupied with prayer alone. To Barlaam's claim that one should force the intellect to separate itself from bodily activities in noetic prayer, Palamas retorts that to cause the noetic faculty to wander outside the body in order to seek intelligible visions is the source and root of Greek errors and all heresies, an invention of demons.[12]

The *whole of man* was meant to be purified and to participate in the divine nature, not simply the mind (or any other human faculty capable of being severed from the rest of one's being). This is the Orthodox understanding of the incarnation.

> In those who practice prayer, the action of mind, consisting of thoughts, is easily purified; but the soul which gives birth to these thoughts will not become pure unless at the same time all its other powers are purified.[13]
> So . . . in those who [properly] direct their minds towards God and devote their soul to the desire of the Divine, even their flesh, being transformed, rises up with them and takes part in Divine Communion, whereby it too becomes a possession of God and His house and ceases to harbour "enmity against God" and to lust "against the spirit" (Rom. 8:7 and Gal. 5:17).[14]

St. Gregory's final step in the defense of the (external) hesychastic practices is a simple consequence of the properly understood relationship between the physical (outer) and nonphysical (inner) aspects of man.

---

(12) John S. Romanides, "Notes on the Palamite Controversy and Related Topics—II," *Greek Orthodox Theological Review* 9:2 (1963-1964) 225-270.

(13) Kadloubovsky and Palmer, p. 410.

(14) Ibid., p. 407.

One of the great teachers says that since the fall the inner man usually accords with the outer (with outer movements and postures). If this be so, why not accept it that a man who strives to turn his mind within is greatly helped in this if, instead of letting his eyes wander hither and thither, he turns them inwards and fixes them in his breast?[15]

Not only the eyes, but all of the body should participate in the spiritual practices, since:

Is it not the flesh where, as the Apostle says, "dwelleth no good thing" (Rom. 7:18) until man has received the "law of the spirit of life" (Rom. 8:2)? Therefore it is all the more needful not to leave it without attention. Otherwise how will it be ours. . . ? How can we repulse the attacks of the evil one . . . if we do not learn to keep attention in ourselves by external methods also?[16]

St. Gregory further notes that these external practices are not simply something appropriate to neophytes:

For even the most perfect seer of God, Elijah, "stooped to the ground, and put his face between his knees" (3 Kings 18:42) [I Kings in RSV], and thus collecting his mind within and cleaving with it to God, he broke the drought of many years.[17]

In conclusion, one can only remark that it is a tragedy that Dom Davis Knowles bypassed this opportunity to do justice to a badly neglected field. St. Gregory's defense of hesychasm (and hesychastic practice itself) offers the westerner a greatly needed insight into Orthodox spirituality—a spirituality that is unquestionably in accord with "true evangelical mysticism."

(15) Ibid., p. 406.
(16) Ibid., p. 407.
(17) Ibid.

5

St. Gregory Palamas on the Hesychasts

by

ARCHIMANDRITE CHRYSOSTOMOS

In the Orthodox Church we set aside the second Sunday of Great Lent to honor the memory of the fourteenth-century Archbishop of Thessalonica, St. Gregory Palamas. We laud this miracle-working saint as a pillar of the Church ("Ekklesias to sterigma") and as a great luminary ("Orthodoxias ho phoster") in our hymns. And again on November 14, so important is his contribution to the exposition of the mystical tradition, the Church calls to memory this remarkable saint. Yet St. Gregory is not well known to the common pious and his study by theologians is scant in comparison to the tomes that have been dedicated to other Church Fathers. In Greece, it was not until the recent past that anyone showed any critical attention toward a collection of the saint's writings. And, greatly owing to his rejection by the West and the proverbial "western captivity" of many Orthodox theologians, some Greek theologians have only a rudimentary familiarity with St. Gregory and his immense importance to Orthodox thought. (Happily, the state of Palamite studies in the Slavic traditions is better developed and more profound.)[1] It is no surprise, then, that considerations of St. Gregory Palamas in the English language are limited and few.[2]

"St. Gregory Palamas on the Hesychasts" is in press in *Diakonia* 5 (1980). Printed by permission.

(1) Thus, the author was pleased to see that the late Archbishop Averky, Rector of the Holy Trinity Russian Orthodox Seminary in Jordanville, New York, used Palamite imagery and references in his awe-inspiring sermons. See, for example, "What is Orthodoxy?"—a sermon by His Eminence, in *Orthodox Life* 26:3 (1976) 1-5.

(2) The most familiar English-language volume on St. Gregory Palamas is, of course, *A Study of Gregory Palamas*, by Fr. John Meyendorff (London: Faith Press, 1974), which originally appeared in French. Its limitations are numerous, and Fr. Meyendorff's misunderstanding of many Palamite concepts and his errors in translation have been brilliantly discussed by Fr. John Romanides, particularly in the second part of his essay. See his "Notes on the Palamite Controversy and Related Topics—II," *Greek Orthodox Theological Reivew* 9:2 (1963-1964) 225-270.

To the Orthodox in America, St. Gregory Palamas remains largely unknown and the object of a liturgical commemoration void of that understanding insight by which the seed of worship blossoms fully into a flower of divine knowledge.

What we wish to do in this short essay is introduce a few of the thoughts of St. Gregory Palamas regarding hesychasm or the monastic tradition by which the mind *(nous)* is cleansed, enlightened, and perfected, as this process is characterized in the *Philokalia*.[3] In so doing we will turn to the richness of the original Greek, not wishing in this endeavor to present a systematic Palamite theology (for what is systematic is too often artificial and begets the limitations to which we have alluded above—note 2), but rather simply hoping to familiarize the reader with some of the pertinent, trenchant observations of St. Gregory. To this end, we will summarize the words of the saint in a short essay entitled, "On the Sacred Hesychasts" ("Hyper ton Hieron Hesychazonton").[4] In this one small example of his works, we find that St. Gregory, though profound and often demanding of us in his thought great attention and care, touches on issues of contemporary import with such clarity and brilliance that we almost unconsciously proclaim his outstanding beauty

The Rev. Professor Georges Florovsky also dedicates the last chapter of his *Bible, Church, Tradition: An Eastern Orthodox View*, vol. 1 of his *Collected Works* (Belmont, Mass.: Nordland, 1972) to a consideration of St. Gregory and the patristic tradition. Unfortunately, the chapter is very short and Fr. Florovsky, with an acute awareness of the West's unfamiliarity with Palamite thought, proceeds with such caution in presenting the saint's "daring" thought that the impact of St. Gregory's thought is almost totally lost. Moreover, in comparison to the other chapters in the book, there is a dearth of primary source references.

A few other texts are also available in English, but again, these presentations are also not free from the same misunderstandings and errors that mark the better-known studies mentioned above.

(3) The *Philokalia* (*Dobrotolyubie* in Russian) is a collection of the writings of the Eastern Fathers on the spiritual practices by which the aspirant achieves *theosis* (divinization), ultimate mystical perfection, and union with God.

(4) *Philokalia*, vol. 4 (Athens: Aster, 1977), pp. 121-31. Translations of some of the writings of St. Gregory have appeared in English, including a translation of St. Gregory's essay on the hesychasts in E. Kadloubovsky and G. E. H. Palmer, trs., *Early Fathers from the Philokalia* (London: Faber and Faber, 1969). Most of these translations are very inadequate, and the Kadloubovsky and Palmer translation omits much of the original text and uses a vocabulary that more often than not obscures the depth of the Greek text.

for the spiritual aspirant ("ton monaston he kallone").

In our spiritually barren times, we lack those great "stars" of holy asceticism by which spiritual strugglers in the past, both monastics and pious laymen, guided their ascetic practices. We lack the perfect examples to emulate and therefore often lose sight of the very goals of our endeavors. So it is that we hear more and more often the accusation that monastic asceticism presupposes a kind of hate of the body, a denial of the very substance of the flesh. Having lost so many times the very purposes of our acts, we the religious give by our ignorance and our misguided (or unguided) efforts substance to such accusations. And, sadly enough, many of us begin to embrace such thought and abandon, for want of justification, the ascetic life on the grounds that it just might, indeed, involve an unconscionable rejection of the very flesh which St. Paul calls the dwelling place of the Holy Spirit. But this great confusion comes to us because we do not essentially understand the relationship between the body and the mind and because, by tradition in the West and by improper learning in the East,[5] we have tended to seek, outside of our own bodies and in a frenzied searching for the ecstatic, divine knowledge, setting aside and reviling the immediacy of the flesh. And bound up with this tragic process is the tendency, when the ecstatic is not attained or is even unsatisfying, to cast aside ascetic discipline as abnormal.

In St. Gregory's essay on the hesychasts, he decisively points out for us the importance of the body and its quintessential role in the cleansing of the mind and the attainment of perfection. In so doing, we begin to understand the ascetic life (with its common disciplines of fasting, prayer, vigils, etc.), not as a means merely of casting off the body, but of preparing it for the interaction with the mind that forms the foundation of spiritual enlightenment. In St. Gregory we find that perfect harmony

(5) Fr. Romanides notes that the eastern "mystic" (a term used here with caution) does not seek a life of contemplation as such and does not seek visions. Rather, he simply emphasizes *praxis* (ascetic practice). And while there is, for the eastern "mystic," an ecstatic union with God, this is not the ecstatic experience of the West (as championed by St. Gregory's famous adversary, Barlaam the Calabrian), in which the intellect is raised up and beyond the body. See Romanides, pp. 225-232 passim.

of mind and body in which ascetic practice becomes, not a negative struggle, but a positive instrument. Although St. Gregory's essay is specifically aimed at answering certain objections to the hesychastic method,[6] we find these fruitful answers shining with brilliant hope to the modern monk, as though they were written specifically in response to the problem of mind and body as we have posed it above.

St. Gregory introduces his short essay with an inquiry posed to him by a certain brother regarding calumnies against the hesychasts to the effect that they were wrong in their meditative methods, in that they tried to keep their minds controlled and free from wandering outside the body. The saint begins his commentary with the stern warning that one must not think the body evil, and makes effusive allusions to biblical and patristic texts to the effect that the body is not evil. He cites, as one might expect, the Pauline *dictum* (1 Cor 6:19) that the body is the temple of the Holy Spirit within us ("hoti ta somata hemon naos tou en hemin Hagiou Pneumatos estin").[7] He thus emphasizes that the body is something spiritual, not something to be set aside as unconnected with the spiritual experience. He goes on to point out that it is the preoccupation with things of the flesh which one avoids, not the body itself, the body being the proper vessel for the mind: "Hemeis de en tois somatikois phronemasin einai ton noun oiometha kakon; en to somati de ouchi kakon, epei mede to soma poneron."[8] We see here a very balanced and functional view of the body, a fundamental starting

(6) Many of St. Gregory's writings (such as his essay on the hesychasts) were directed to people who grossly misunderstood the hesychasts and thought that they were teaching a method by which divine grace could be breathed in through the nose ("dia ton mykteron") and by which mere bodily functions could effect divine union. Interestingly, the exchange between St. Gregory and his detractors represents the development of two "mystical traditions," as it were, one emphasizing the instrumental importance of the body, the other considering the body an impediment to spiritual vision. Most of the detractors adhered to the very concepts of the body that led to the unbalanced notion of the relationship between body and mind of the less-productive monastic traditions, the fruits of which we see in much of the contemporary demise of ascetic life.

(7) *Philokalia*, p. 123.
(8) Ibid., p. 124.

point for the hesychasts, which belies the notion that monastic asceticism is necessarily antisomatic.

St. Gregory continues on in his opening remarks to identify just what it is about the flesh that is evil. If it is the dwelling place of the Holy Spirit, it certainly cannot be as such functionally evil, but evil only as it serves other purposes. He notes that St. Paul describes man as sold to sin and asserts that a man sold as a slave is not one by nature ("ou physei doulos").[9] Therefore the postlapsarian body is evil not by nature, but by disposition. Amplifying on the Apostle Paul's statement that within him there dwelled no good, St. Gregory contends that it is not the body which is evil, but that which dwells within it ("hoti ou ten sarka, alla to enoikoun aute, phesi, kakon").[10] Cleansing the body of all sinful thought, we make it the abode of spiritual power, ruled over, appropriately, by the mind, which has become the overseer ("he episkope").[11] The appropriate place for the mind, then, is indeed the body. And the body properly ruled by the mind becomes not an evil thing, but a thing of good.

Once the body has been properly subjected to the mind, St. Gregory writes, a certain triumvirate of principles comes to ascendancy. First, through the discipline of the body, one learns also to control the sensations of the mind. This is called *enkrateia* (literally "temperance") or mastery over the senses. Second, the correct use of the body and the mind allows the soul (or the desiring portion of the soul—"to de pathetiko merei tes psyches")[12] to acquire love. And third, one develops a neptic sobriety, a mental process of cleansing the mind by removing from it all that prevents its elevation toward God. In this triumvirate of principles, in the first instance, the usual interaction between the mind and body typical of normal cognitive functioning is subjected to certain controls. In modern psychological parlance we would say that the mind no longer monitors bodily

(9) Ibid.
(10) Ibid.
(11) Ibid.
(12) Ibid.

sensations as a basis for the formation of thought and action. These sensations ("passions" in the nomenclature of the ascetic Fathers) cease to intercede in the mind's control of the body. And of course essential to this mastery over the passions is ascetic practice, by which the conditioned responses between the passions and the mind ("habit" as the Fathers would call it) are broken. In the second instance, one practices Christian virtues in acts of love and reverence, by which external stimuli are no longer effective in determining behavior; anger and passions offer, rather, the opportunity for virtue.[13] In the last instance, this system avers, the mind is mystically cleansed and stands before God and the aspirant sees within himself the grace of the pure in heart.[14]

When the body is used as a spiritual instrument, it is given great powers, according to Palamite theology, for it becomes the vessel of the mind and, as it were, its proper servant. But what particular part of the body constitutes the mind itself? It is essential here to look at St. Gregory's response. He emphasizes that the mind is contained within the heart, not with the heart as its vessel (for the mind is incorporeal—"asomaton"), but nonetheless as its "repository" ("tameion").[15] It is into the heart, then, that the mind, distracted on all sides normally by the senses, must retreat. It must introduce itself into the repository of thoughts. Quoting St. Makarios the Great, St. Gregory affirms that the mind turned inward to the heart finds there, when the heart is occupied with grace, the laws of the spirit. The heart contains the "throne of grace" ("en to tes charitos throno").[16] We must not overlook here a tradition that St. Gregory Palamas cites. The Eastern Fathers invariably call one to recognize the role of the heart in spiritual enlightenment. This is of utmost importance for any student of hesychasm. Though in a subtle manner, more than any other aspect of hesychastic

---

(13) Ibid., pp. 124-25. This is most beautifully expressed in the Greek.
(14) Ibid., p. 125: "ktatai kai hora en heauto ten epengelmenen charin tois kekatharmenois ten kardian."
(15) Ibid.
(16) ibid.

thought, this emphasis on the heart over and against the brain stresses that neptic control is not something cerebral and not something akin to mere "mind control." In an absolute sense, it is for this reason that hesychastic practice is in fact unrelated to yoga, as some eclectic thinkers would propose. And it is for this reason, too, that one should not confuse simple mental use of the "Jesus Prayer" (the heart of monastic practice), as is unfortunately common today, with prayer contained in the heart. One is cerebral, the other "mystical."

The entry of the mind into the heart constitutes, for St. Gregory, the most important defense of the hesychastic admonition that one must not, in spiritual practice, search for what is outside the body. The heart is that place in which the mind not only collects its thoughts, but in which it examines and reflects upon itself. It enters the Kingdom of God within. The mind, St. Gregory Palamas writes (quoting St. Dionysios the Great), "sees itself" ("heauton ho nous hora").[17] This is an astounding statement, for it suggests a deep self-reflection. But it is all the more astounding when we realize that St. Gregory posits that this self-reflection of the mind takes place within a grace-filled inner chamber. It is not, then, mere self-reflection that is the basis of hesychasm. Nor is it some supracognitive internal self-revelation of the mind that constitutes the hesychastic experience. It is, we sense from these profound statements of St. Gregory, in the confines of the divine presence, outside mental processes as we understand them and in the depths of the heart of man, that true prayer, true communion, and true preparation for union with God take place. Realizing this, we are bereft of any justification in comparing Palamite hesychasm (as is unwisely done all too often by theological dilettantes) to the desultory spiritual experiences that we encounter in contemporary "mysticism," "spiritual encounters," or would-be holy "elders." It is sobering to see the incredible depth of the Palamite experience.

St. Gregory Palamas now returns to the essential question

(17) Ibid., p. 126.

56

that prompted his commentary on the nature of spiritual experience and assures the reader that there must be no doubt as to the efficacy and necessity of turning the mind toward the body (not away from it) and inwardly toward the heart. And this inward movement, we are assured, often results in the mind being returned to itself, freed from external concerns, and therefore by nature ascending to union with God. The hesychast is thus unified with God, not by seeking something outside of himself or by taking the mind away from the body, but by placing the mind within the depths of the body, within the heart. In so doing, in confining the mind within itself, the hesychast becomes, ironically, an incorporeal being. St. Gregory quotes an amazing statement by St. John of the Ladder to this effect: "hos hesychastes estin ho to asomaton en somati periorizein speudon."[18] We are further assured by this holy and enlightened Father that all of the Fathers have taught this same truth.[19]

The remainder of St. Gregory's essay is aimed at a defense of the various physical practices by which the inner and outer man (the mind and the body, in some sense) are brought into proper relationship, in preparation for the entry of the mind into

(18) Ibid, p. 127. This difficult passage is adequately, though with great license, translated by Kadloubovsky and Palmer as follows: "The hesychast is an incorporeal being who strives to keep his soul within the limits of its bodily home."

(19) This seems to be an appropriate place to add an incidental remark. We see in St. Gregory an assertion that his teachings are those taught by all of the Fathers. Indeed, his writings are nothing more nor less than a *compendium* of the mystical teachings of the Fathers, compiled in such a way as to present in one place a system otherwise scattered through many texts. This point is one which eludes some ill-read commentators on St. Gregory, who find in him a "new Orthodoxy," a "new dimension" of eastern theological thought. Such discoveries are spurious and result from a poor understanding of the spiritual tradition of the Fathers.

One cannot help but note this trend toward finding "new theologies" and "new dimensions" in Orthodoxy—as though, contrary to what spiritual experience teaches and the Church affirms, there is not an unbroken tradition of Orthodox wisdom which disallows the sudden creation of a "new" system. (By this, however, we do not suggest that Orthodox tradition is dead conservatism. Far from it!) This trend has resulted in some ridiculous characterizations of Serafim of Sarov, the great Russian saint. And it reaches a truly ludicrous level when one finds scholars suggesting that the Orthodox Church is not known by this name and as a distinct entity before the Great Schism, as an otherwise competent scholar recently commented. This trend, which results from the poor state of some aspects of patristic scholarship, should be checked. Not only are its scholarly foundations faulty, but it is spiritually harmful.

the heart. There are rich allusions to the mystical writings of the Fathers and to the hesychastic practices of specific champions of those practices: St. Symeon the New Theologian and his contemporaries, as well as other great Church Fathers. While the development of this portion of the essay is no less essential and no less captivating than the portions which we have covered, we will leave it to a subsequent paper to discuss the practice of hesychasm, which must be approached with great care, lest the neophyte find in this practice a source of self-instruction.[20] Suffice it to say that our present remarks touch, though briefly, on subjects of deep import which, in and of themselves, demand great attention and contemplation.

We find, in St. Gregory Palamas, a dimension of spiritual insight so profound and so striking that we are, true to his very own words, compelled to receive them as the food of a spiritual experience of the deepest kind. In so receiving them, the ascetic life of the monk takes on a significance and an immediacy that mere speculation about the prerequisites of divine union theorized in contemplative systems can never offer. In St. Gregory there is theory pregnant with true experience. We read in the *Evergetinos* a beautiful little statement that sums up the soul's reaction to the profound experiences of St. Gregory: "Another wise Father compares one who teaches with words, without doing works, to a tree which has leaves but does not bear fruit."[21] The soul delights in the wonderful foliage of St. Gregory's words and yet feasts on the sumptuous nourishment of the God-bearing fruit which his works of wonder produce.

(20) Indeed, no one should embark on hesychastic practice without rigid training and the guidance of a spiritual father—a guidance which no monk, in this spiritually vapid age, would be wise to offer.

(21) *Mikros Evergetinos* (Athens: Agion Oros, 1977), p. 30.

6
Some Thoughtful Comments on Orthodox Meditation

ARCHIMANDRITE CHRYSOSTOMOS AND
HIERODEACON AKAKIOS

It has been some time since Dr. James Counelis offered his short article, "Twelve Festal Meditations," to the readers of *Diakonia*.[1] During this passage of three years, we have wanted to use his observations as a platform from which to discuss common misconceptions of meditation in Orthodox thought. Hopefully, the detachment afforded by these years will emphasize that our comments are not meant to be *ad hominem* in nature. At no moment have we doubted the sincerity with which Dr. Counelis proffered the fruits of his personal devotion. Nor have we doubted that many of his observations were, indeed, noteworthy. It is simply that the common notions about eastern prayer perpetuated in his remarks are so clear and precise that one cannot resist the benefits gained in using his short meditations as an outline for a response to a spiritual weakness in our comprehension of true prayer—a weakness which we, Dr. Counelis, and all men in our spiritually dry century share.

The concepts of prayer and meditation that abound in our times are too eclectic and insufficiently immersed in the profound struggle that the understanding of any *truly* spiritual tradition demands. These misapprehensions not only becloud the whole of the eastern witness, but they lead Orthodox, in America especially—where a reliable substructure of mature spiritual Fathers and spiritual guides is virtually unknown (however much the admission of this fact may annoy and convict us)—to distorted views of classical patristic *praxis*. So it is that we have Christians finding in the labors of the Fathers analogs of the more recent experiences of the contemporary charismatics, and

---

"Some Thoughtful Comments on Orthodox Meditation" appeared in *Diakonia* 14:2 (1979) 151-157. Reprinted by permission.
(1) *Diakonia* 11:1 (1976) 34-41.

non-Orthodox seeing with their own eyes phenomena which the Fathers saw through quite a different visional faculty. By the same token, we find those who would in some way offer their own spiritual experience, in however commendably self-effacing a manner, as consistent with (albeit acknowledgedly inferior to) that of the Fathers.

Why are our experiences and those of the Fathers sometimes of a different kind? And why must we be careful not to draw parallels between our own religious experiences and those of the Fathers? The answer to the first question is painfully evident in a thorough reading of the Fathers. The Abbot Sisois, for example, is often cited for his mastery of the art of repentance. He spent his entire life weeping for his fallen nature and, at his death, felt that there was still much to learn in that art. Yet there are those who claim assurance of salvation and mastery of repentance some days, if not hours, after a mere verbal confession of faith. Are the experiences of the holy abbot and these latter experiences to be compared? Are we, in the same strain, to compare the experiences of the Apostle Paul, which he could not even utter (2 Cor 12:4), to the free-flowing testimonies that abound in many forms of charismatic worship? We think not.

The Fathers speak of incredible struggle and effort in attaining the divine life, of the many trials which the spiritual life generates and of the loathesome pitfalls which *prelest* (spiritual pride or delusion, as the Russians call it) can visit upon the aspirant after the *vie spirituelle*. The Fathers worked for salvation in the deserts and barren places of the earth for seemingly endless years, enduring hardships of kinds we can only barely imagine. They knew the folly of the "ten minute" conversion and they knew the gruesome warfare with nature itself that leads to theosis.

Likewise, the Holy Fathers knew the true joy of spiritual vision, of the unspeakable wonder of the gifts of God. But these joys, this wonderment, cannot, as Bishop Ignaty Brianchaninov so strikingly states in his guide to spiritual practice, *The Arena*, be compared to the joys of daily life, to the joys experienced by our normal media of cognition, even if these joys reach their highest possible experssions.[2] Again we find this theme in St. John the Carpathian, who speaks of the highest spiritual joy of the monk amidst daily experiences of sorrow, temptation, and suffering. Indeed, *hypomone* and *kairos* (patience and time) are the bywords of the ascent to divinization, not earthly joy and running through fields of flowers, hand-in-hand, with brotherly love. The final spiritual vision, attained sometimes after years of spiritual struggle and ascetic labor, is not accessible to the mind of man, but to a *phronema pneumatikon* (spiritual mind), to the noetic faculty. It is to be seen, as the Fathers often paradoxically note, with a vision that is not vision as we understand it.

To be sure, the experiences of the Fathers can be ours. But such an affirmation, especially in our times, must be made with great caution and unending reservations. However, the Fathers must never appear to us as mad; they suffered, not out of some psychological aberration, but because their struggles were and are the sine qua non for enlightenment. It is we who are mad if we think that this age-old witness can be replaced with "easier methods" adapted to our own age, in which the arrogance of man at his technological "highest" lulls us into the false assumption that somehow our natures do not demand of us the same discipline and rigor which the Fathers displayed in their work for salvation.

This statement is harsh, but it is necessary. And by it we come upon our second question, regarding the danger of thinking that our own spiritual experiences are, in fact, at one with those of the Fathers, in that mystical *consensus patrum*[3] which insures the catholicity of the Christian experience. Such a thought should not occur unless our own experiences arise out of years of physical and spiritual torment and labor—from *asketike er-*

---

(2) A translated passage from Bishop Ignaty to this effect can be found in a very provocative editorial essay, "A Man Is His Faith," *Nikodemos* 4 (1975) 12.

(3) Thus it is that we find the staretz Paisii referring to the Fathers as speaking "as though with one mouth." See Elder Paisius Velichkovsky, "To a Uniate Priest, On the Procession of the Holy Spirit," *Orthodox Word* (September-October 1975), p. 203.

gasia. And then, too, our experiences, to parallel those of the Fathers, must be in perfect harmony with them: not by the detail of the word, but by the spirit of the word, with the *phronema* and *kerygma* of the Fathers. And since the bulk of this spirit comes to us, as St. Basil say, "en mysterio," one would expect silence from the true holy man. How few can lay claim to such qualifications. How few would dare to do so!

We turn, then, to Dr. Counelis' meditations. Why are they objectionable? Simply because an Orthodox Christian is compelled, if he wishes to follow the Fathers in his quest for spiritual knowledge, to avoid Counelis' "cerebral, rational, and contemplative sense" (p. 34). And this not because the Fathers are to be blindly followed out of some notion of conservatism in which independent or rational thought is to be spurned, but because the Fathers knew the source and ramifications of such a "sense." As St. Mark the Ascetic warns us to put ourselves "truly above all sensory and mental things,"[4] so St. Gregory Palamas affirms that seeking after intelligible visions is the "source and root" of errors and is demonic.[5] And "the Hesychasts knew," one writer observes, "what the consequences of ecstatic, extracorporal experiences were."[6]

To let the mind wander into creative and uncommon visions, however elevating an experience this might be for the poet, is to the spiritual man utter disaster. The separation of the body and intellect (or *praxis* and *theoria,* for that matter) is a violation of the synergy between the body and the mind which marks Orthodox spirituality. In short, cerebral contemplation that eschews or ignores the perfect cooperation by grace of the body

(4) See this passage in E. Kadloubovsky and G. E. H. Palmer, trs., *Early Fathers from the Philokalia* (London: Faber and Faber, 1969), p. 78.

(5) These references by St. Gregory can be found in an excellent essay on Palamite theology (designed as a critical response to Fr. John Meyendorff's *A Study of Gregory Palamas,* London: Faith Press, 1974). See Fr. John Romanides, "Notes on the Palamite Controversy and Related Topics—II," *Greek Orthodox Theological Review* 9:2 (1963-1964) 232.

(6) Hieromonk Auxentios, "Dom David Knowles on Hesychasm: A Palamite Rejoinder," published as chapter 4 of the present volume. This essay offers some trenchant observations regarding Orthodox prayer and takes Dom Knowles to task for his surprisingly subjective and unscholarly treatment of hesychasm.

and mind, which the ascetic practices of the Fathers strive to attain, is not likely to engender that "Divine Communion" of which St. Gregory Palamas speaks.[7]

The Fathers spoke from a level beyond the mere rational. As St. John Chrysostom says of St. Paul, he spoke "by the spirit."[8] It is this spiritual manner of speaking, passed down "apo tes siopomenes kai mystikes paradoseos" ("from the silent and mystical tradition"),[9] which underlies the tradition of Orthodox literature. Thus it is that St. Romanos the Melodist, that spirit-drenched poet of the Eastern Church, cried out his praise not from contemplative concentration or even from creative insight, but from the transcendent faith which, as St. Athanasios describes it, "ho kyrios edoken" ("the Lord gave"), "hoi apostoloi ekeryxan" ("the Apostles preached"), and "hoi pateres ephylaxan" ("the Fathers preserved").[10] Indeed, meditation in the Orthodox Church is nothing less than a transcendence of the cognitive, of the cerebral, and of the rational as we know them. It is a participation in that mind of Christ to which St. Paul alludes (1 Cor 2:16), a mind that perceives not from the "knowledge of words and man's wisdom," but from "the teaching of the Spirit" ("en didaktois pneumatos"— 1 Cor 2:13).

It is interesting to note here, parenthetically, that even the spiritual formulas that the Church herself gives us are not, *simply* by the words themselves, efficacious. Even those words and thoughts coming from outside our own minds have an ultimate inner significance and goal. A fine example of this is a lesson well known to spiritual elders. As the story goes, a man was entrusted to an abusive elder who refused to tonsure him until he learned the salutation to the Theotokos ("Virgin Theotokos, rejoice, Mary full of Grace, the Lord is with Thee; blessed art Thou among women and blessed is the fruit of Thy womb, for

(7) Kadloubovsky and Palmer, p. 407.
(8) Philipp Schaff, ed., *A Select Library of the Nicene and Post-Nicene Fathers*, first series, vol. 13 (New York, 1889), p. 36.
(9) St. Basil the Great, *Peri tou Pneumatos*, PG 32:188.
(10) PG 26:595-96.

Thou hast borne the Savior of our souls"). After many trials and after much abuse from the elder, the aspirant died, having learned nothing more, over the years, than the words "Chaire Maria" ("Rejoice Mary"). In time, a rose bush grew over the man's grave and on each petal of the blossoms there appeared the words, "Rejoice Mary." Upon exhuming the body, the abusive elder and his followers found the roots of the rose bush implanted in the aspirant's heart. In this way we learn that not only are we to receive divinity in detachment from all personal thought and opinion, but that, if God so honors the humility underlying such a dispensation, the very words given to us by tradition have within them a power and a message that transcend the words themselves. Verbalism never suffices to contain the Christian truth.

When we write from mere reason, therefore, we fail to capture the Christian experience. Emotion, another attribute of the reasonable being, is equally incapable of grasping the truth. Whether from reason or emotion, when we write with our own thoughts before us, we tend to see divine things in a mundane, unnatural way—attributing to this vision the notion of "natural" as fallen man conceives of it. Thus, Dr. Counelis sees the magnificently mystical Akathist hymn as free from the Freudian imagery of eroticism because it is essentially a teaching hymn that portrays for us the honor due Mary as the vessel "through whom wisdom came down to us" (p. 36). If, however, one senses that the hymn is a theological discourse on the image of man's salvation by virtue of the birth of Christ within him, the apparently Freudian symbolism takes on a new meaning. To the man immersed in spiritual life, in the process of giving birth "in a non-bodily way" ("asomatos") to Christ, of becoming another "Mother of God" (as St. Maximos the Confessor speaks of the incarnation and the Theotokos), the imagery has a rich, full expression in his experiences. He receives the words as perfect projections of his struggle and hope, not in an exalted sense of theological insight, but as icons of his emerging spiritual mind. The possibility of Freudian interpretations are as remote

64

from his vision as the vision of God is from the man immersed in Freudian symbolism.

In meditation five (p. 37f.), Counelis proclaims the mystery of death as the gateway to life, owing to the victory of Christ over man's enemy par excellence. With the reasoning of a human mind, he proclaims this a mystery, a mystery which the human spirit only fully comes to understand, at the second coming. Yet the very message of the Church, the very spirit of the Liturgy, and the very encounter with the divine are foretastes of the life which is free from death. To a man freed from human thought, death is a mystery of a much different kind. The witness of the Fathers teaches us that they know well the antecedents of death and what follows it. The mystery is this knowledge itself, which cannot be adequately conveyed to the human mind. It is not, as our logic would tell us, the fearful ignorance we have of the mystery of death. One walking in spiritual knowledge knows, partially even here on earth, divinity. Thus it is that saints, so caught up in divinity while dwelling among us, drench, as it were, their very bones with divinity, leaving, in their relics, evidence of new matter, or a miraculous substance, of the world filled with grace. It is the reception of this divinity here on earth that is the mystery.

In a summary expression, we hear Dr. Counelis pronounce that "Transcendence is the continuum between the antipodes of man's prayer and Divine Providence" (p. 41). We have amply shown that transcendence is not, in fact, a quality of the acts of man. It is not part of a continuum at all. It exists above time, above the primary category by which we conceive of the continuum. And even the synergy between God and man, we have hinted, is not an exact formula, in which this or that element, like an enzyme and its substrate, matches another to evoke a spiritual result.

At times, by the grace of God, even this synergy is inadequate to express spiritual enlightenment (as in the case of the aspirant who could not learn a prescribed prayer of the Church, and yet glorified the Mother of God with miraculous wonder).

Our rational thoughts, even our "theological" truths, cannot adequately grasp that which is above thought. And much less can we hope to ascend to spiritual knowledge by indulging our own personal experiences. Through the guidelines of the Church, our efforts are patterned, dictated, and orchestrated by the witness of the Fathers who have gone before us. Even one word of our personal thought is unwise. And then God, in his own ineffable way, gives to us freely his grace, neither as a reward for our work nor actually as the result of synergy, the wisdom to know what our knowledge cannot even perceive. This is ture meditation and this is the true wisdom by which "even the most authentic appearing *staretz*" (p.34) *does* in fact attain the freedom of which Christ speaks (St. John 8:32). Free from mere thought and personal opinion, the true *staretz* finds the Truth which sets him free.

7

Cultural *Paradosis* and Orthodox America

by

ARCHIMANDRITE CHRYSOSTOMOS

We are accustomed to seeing the Greek word *paradosis,* or tradition, as a touchstone of Orthodox theology. What the Lord gave us, what the Holy Apostles preached, and what the Fathers of the Church preserved, as St. Athanasios expressed it, are the very foundations of what we call Orthodoxy—they are its "tradition." Tradition expresses truth. All opinion, speculation, and creativity in theological thought must be measured against the criterion of Holy Tradition. Given the singular ascendancy of the concept of tradition for the Orthodox Christian, then, we might be startled at the words "cultural *paradosis.*" After all, Holy Tradition is something meant for all times, for all places, and for all peoples. Holy Tradition, Orthodoxy itself, is somehow above culture. Its frame of reference is not only existential, but precisely away from the mere human culture. It draws us toward that nonearthly "homeland" to which St. John Chrysostom calls us. How, indeed, can the Orthodox Christian give serious attention to the concerns of cultural tradition, given the preeminent imperatives presented by Holy Tradition?

If we are startled at the notion of a cultural *paradosis,* our shock might well reflect a certain spiritual malaise which we Americans, being so young in our Orthodoxy, tend all too often to ignore or to fail to discover in ourselves. An anecdote from the ancient desert Fathers might help us to understand this spiritual foible. A young spiritual aspirant was once allowed by his elder to go into the city. On his journey he passed a magnificent monastery where he heard the brothers speaking of great and marvelous theological precepts. He thought to himself how humble and unimportant his own spiritual life was, centered, as it was, around the simple practice of the Jesus Prayer ("Lord Jesus Christ, Son of God, have mercy on me a sinner"). Returning to his elder, he expressed his marvel at the monastery he had seen on his journey to the city. His elder, a man of great spiritual power, summoned the young monk after some time and directed him to make another journey into the city. The aspirant obediently followed his elder's directions and set out for the city. It happened that, just as he came to the monastery that he had seen on his previous visit, the earth began to tremble. Fearing the earthquake, the monks of the monastery poured out of their cells in full sight of the traveling aspirant. As they fled, the young traveler heard each monk say, "Jesus Christ, Son of God, have mercy on me a sinner." Foreseeing the earthquake, the monk's elder had sent him on this journey to learn a profound lesson.

And what did the young monk learn? He learned that long before one may speak of great theological precepts, one must know basic spiritual practice. Without the foundation of personal spiritual experience, the great structure of theological theory cannot stand. And if the structure of theological theory begins to fall, the final refuge of the mature Christian is that personal spiritual practice. In the moment of crisis, it was not to high-sounding theology that the city monks had turned, but to the simplicity of the practice that the desert monk embraced. So it is that here in America we tend to look at Orthodoxy's exalted Holy Tradition, taking pride in our knowledge of Orthodox history, dogma, and doctrine, all the while forgetting that this tradition has reached us through historical reality, through our forefathers, through our cultural *paradosis*. To know Orthodoxy as the "cultureless" culture, as timeless Holy Tradition, we must first know it as it is practically given to us: through the customs, habits, and worldviews of our Orthodox forefathers, be they Greek, Russian, Serbian, Rumanian, Bulgarian, Syrian, or whatever.

The "Old Country" Phenomenon. Any Orthodox Christian in America is for a moment discomforted by the notion that the things of the "old Country" are somehow essential to his reception of Orthodoxy itself. But this discomfort comes to us because social realities have for some time prevented most of us from reflecting maturely and objectively on our cultural heritage. From early Greek settlements in Nebraska to Slavic communities in the eastern urban centers, almost all Orthodox have felt the sting of prejudice and, to some extent, social alienation. Our natural inclination has been to blend into the American social fabric and to accommodate those traits which make us suspect to the more prevailing culture. This blending and this accommodation have brought a certain acceptance to Orthodox in America, and one recoils at the thought of losing that safe social status. But we must realize that, more importantly, we have paid a great price in losing many of the things that our cultural oddities brought, not the least of which is a certain subtle Orthodox spirit which permeated the "old country" mentality and traditions. Realizing this, we must now use the relative safety our assimilation into American life has afforded us as a sense of security in which we can regain freely much of what we have lost.

Orthodoxy is a way of life, a spiritual path, by which the whole of the human creature is caught up in divinity, transformed, united to Christ, and created anew. In the hesychastic tradition of the Church, we are constantly struck with the notion that the mind and its thoughts, the body and its actions, the individual and society are somehow basically integrated. Their correct and harmonious interactions are the very expressions of spiritual attainment. Orthodoxy, then, is more than a religion or the organization of a religious community; it is at once a human culture and a divine manifestation. As the Byzantines beautifully envisaged human society (a vision so terribly distorted by prejudice and misunderstanding in western historiography), it expressed in human dimensions the magnificence and beauty of paradise. In the *pleroma* of the Orthodox experience, society (be it the microcosmic society of a church community or the macrocosmic Orthodox imperial societies of Byzantium or Russia), in its ideal expression, lifts up the mundane and unites it to the heavenly in synergy and image. No single culture serves itself, but serves to express the Eternal Orthodox Culture.

69

And, as Khomiakov so beautifully phrased it, man ceases to be an isolated, alienated individual; he is lifted up in the whole, saved only together with others, damned only in his individuality.

The "old country" mentality and tradition preserved much of this higher view of Orthodoxy in daily life. How seldom we think that the very foods passed down by our "old country" cultures are not simply foods created by individual taste and topography. Not at all. They are foods which developed according to the canons of the church fasts. They are foods (e.g., *kulich* among the Russians, *vasilopita* among the Greeks, and wheat and honey in all Orthodox nationalities) that surround a great celebration of the Church, often expressing even a theological understanding of some particular feast day or church service (as in the case of boiled wheat to represent the resurrection of the dead at memorial services for the departed). Individual taste is largely set aside to serve the eternal truths of the faith. Food is raised up from the mundane and made holy. Likewise in customs of dress we transcend personal taste and exalt the spiritual. Not so much out of morbidity do Orthodox traditionally mourn the dead by wearing black clothing, but out of an understanding that death must be always remembered and present to us in order to balance our reception of life. We are drawn by the mourning families, who are visible to us, into an understanding of our common fate. And we are further motivated to seek our comfort and hope, not in the passing tastes of society, but in events (such as death) which must guide our social lives. And then, too, in the traditional dress of the clergy (which is lamentably almost unknown here in America) we see before us the image of the Patriarchs and Prophets who call us away from the temporal to the enduring things of eternity. In the "old country" culture we find ourselves immersed in that blending of the spiritual and the mundane which should be the everyday Orthodox experience, not the experience of an Orthodoxy which we are ever faster relegating to the Sunday service.

We must say here, too, something about traditional Orthodox culture and language. Perhaps nowhere else do we have a more unbalanced view of what it means to be Orthodox and to be American. With fierce emotions we often proclaim the right of English-speaking Orthodox to have the services in their own language, decrying the use of the traditional languages as the source of every ill in the Church: the young people do not understand the services; the essence of Orthodoxy is lost because of an incomprehensible Liturgy. What we must first understand is that Americans do, indeed, have a right to the Liturgy in English. But this right must be asserted and claimed correctly. If our young do not want to hear the Orthodox message, the use of English will solve nothing. (The experience of English-speaking parishes suggest in many cases that this contention is correct.) Those who truly want to know the Church at a deeper level would never abandon the Church because of language. All of us can in a few months learn enough of the liturgical languages in our Churches to understand the basic nature of the services. Moreover, good Greek-English, Slavonic-English, Arabic-English, and other parallel texts are readily available. We must not confuse those who would use language as an excuse to flee their responsibilities to learn their faith with those who want a deeper understanding of the faith they already feel in their hearts through their own tongue.

Nor should we forget that the traditional liturgical languages cannot be abandoned altogether. To seek repentance in the Orthodox Church does not carry along with it the same implications and meaning that such a quest has for the Protestant or Roman Catholic. We can use, then, for example, an understanding of the Greek word *metanoia* (a changing of mind or outlook) to express the particularly Orthodox view of repentance. Our traditional language has come to serve us theologically; it has become something more than a mere language. In the same way, the Slavonic language (and other Orthodox liturgical languages) have preserved words that perfectly express Orthodox theological notions unknown in the West or misleading in translation. If, as civilized individuals, we at least recognize the importance of knowing other languages in learning of other people, we should not abandon a clear recognition of the fact

71

that Orthodoxy, too, speaks its own languages. We should know these. And finally, we must never think that the services themselves are merely literal. If our traditional languages can serve us, they also have their limits. The most authentic experience of the Liturgy and the church services, after all, takes place noetically, mystically, outside time and space. The truest form of Orthodox worship comes to us through our culture and then transcends form, image, and all dimensions of the literal. We are transported to a new realm, where language, expression, and human action have an altogether different content and intent.

If we wish to attain to the highest understanding of Orthodoxy, there is no doubt that we have to draw on the "old country" cultures which expressed this understanding. If America has a culture (and many sociologists and anthropologists would argue that it does not), that culture is not Orthodox. It was not created to serve the Orthodox *Weltansicht*. It is in many ways incompatible with the Orthodox view. In time, perhaps, an Orthodox culture might grow up in America. But at this juncture, we have no choice but to retreat, whether temporarily or permanently, to those cultures which were shaped by their interaction with the holy. We must regain the priceless crucible in which our divine saints and Holy Fathers were formed. As difficult as it may be for us Orthodox in America to understand, the true expression of our faith does demand the rejection of much of the witless, plastic, and soul-destroying mediocrity of American society. This may mean, ultimately, a change in our styles of dress, in our manner of eating, and in our general self-presentation. But this, after all, is what Orthodoxy is: what we eat, how we speak, how we stand, how we sit, indeed how we understand ourselves and others. If we succeed in regaining this view and this cultural tradition, the benefits may accrue, not only to us, but to America itself.

Converts and Orthodox Culture. Regaining our Orthodox cultural traditions is crucial for those Americans who received their Orthodoxy from their emigrant forefathers. But if it is crucial for those with at least some exposure to that tradition, it is for the convert to Orthodoxy in America a sine qua non of successful growth in Orthodoxy that he adopt many of these same cultural traditions. In many instances we have failed at teaching the growing number of converts to Orthodoxy in this country the fulness of the Orthodox experience. We have touched them with a surface-level Orthodoxy, forming our witness into something akin to a doctrinal or theological alternative to the prevailing Western Christian traditions to which most Americans adhere. In effect, not wholly grasping ourselves the fulness of the Orthodox experience, we have presented the convert population with a religious alternative modeled on a non-Orthodox scheme. The result is that many converts live with an incomplete Orthodoxy, lacking even the partial exposure to Orthodoxy as a culture that the offspring of Orthodox emigrants experience. They cannot even intuit in most cases this fuller Orthodoxy. Such an Orthodoxy cannot fully serve them and stands to suffer from the same foibles as the prevalent Christian witnesses, lacking as they do a full integration of their theological precepts and religious consciousness into daily life, into cultural tradition—an integration which Orthodoxy holds up at its practical means of transmitting the faith to generation after generation.

The convert might object, indeed, to the thought of having to adopt an Orthodox culture as a prerequisite for the reception of the Orthodox faith. "Must I become a Greek, or a Russian, or a Serbian, or so on?" might be the rhetorical response to this prerequisite. The answer is, to some extent, "yes." That we separate Orthodoxy from its cultural medium is already evidence that we have lost a great dimension of Orthodoxy, as we have said. But just as importantly, it is essential to remember that conversion to a true Christianity is the denial of secular culture, the acceptance of a new culture formed by detachment from the world and Christian involvement in it—St. Paul's paradoxical state of being "in" but not "of" the world. This new culture is the very culture which Orthodox societies, however successfully or unsuccessfully, have attempted to build. We are bound by the Christian experience to accept and follow those attempts.

73

They are our one step out of the world while being in it. American society, not built on these same attempts, is not compatible with Orthodoxy. The realization of this heavy and stark reality is no more threatening to us than it was to the Greeks (and subsequently all other Orthodox peoples) when they gave up their pagan cultures and accepted the Christian culture of the Hellenic world.

It is not too much, thus, to ask of the convert that he remain loyal to his country (rendering unto Caesar that which is Caesar's) while, at the same time, adopting a new culture and new traditions better suited to the expression and preservation of his Orthodox faith. This is not a restrictive requirement, but one which brings the Orthodox convert spiritually into a new dimension as well as intellectually into contact with some of the most profound pillars of the edifice of human civilization. The adoption of traditional styles of eating and dress lends itself to the expression of Orthodox spirituality. It provides a context in which association with the secularized world is predefined from an Orthodox stance. And it provides, at the same time, knowledge of the Christian ancients, of Greek and Slavic civilization, and of the deep, theologically developed languages in which the Truth of truths was articulated. To be sure, an adoption of a traditional Orthodox culture expands the American convert to Orthodoxy in every way, the end result being, perhaps sometime in the future, the actual creation of a particularly American expression of these cultures.

We might note here that in one other way the Orthodox convert is called to a mature view of Orthodox cultural traditions. If it is essential that some cultural medium for the expression and preservation of Orthodoxy be realized, it is equally essential that the constant emphasis in this realization is on medium and purpose, not on the cultural traditions as ends in themselves. All too often in our age of the "coy primitive," a few "converts" are attracted to Orthodoxy by the very cultural traditions to which most converts lack essential exposure. These individuals find the "different" ways of the Orthodox strangely appealing or "quaint." They too lack exposure to true Orthodox cultural traditions, for these traditions separated from the spiritual purposes that they serve are false traditions. And anyone converted on such a basis is not converted to the lifegiving essence of Orthodoxy, but to cultural dilettantism. Orthodox cultural traditions are lifted up and participate in the holy only because they serve the Orthodox Christian in his divine ascent and in his simple attempts to live a pious, peaceful, and Christian life on earth. As such they are invaluable. As simple human traditions, they have no meaning to the Christian. In their spirit, these traditions help the aspirant in his God-pleasing life; by their letter, they lead to the perdition of merely human thought and taste.

The Parameters of Genuine Orthodox Culture. It is perhaps auspicious that we began this essay with reference, not to simple tradition, but to Holy Tradition and its expression through Orthodox cultural traditions. In so doing, we have made spiritual considerations paramount in our references to those traditions. Just as the Orthodox convert must receive the cultural medium of the Orthodox faith in the sense of that culture's facilitation of spiritual growth and maturity, we must emphasize boldly the responsibility of those born to Orthodox cultures (whether in the native cultural environment or in diaspora) to receive those aspects of their cultural traditions which are indeed designed to serve spiritual needs. Cultural traditions can lose the spiritual dimension which originally engendered them. But at the same time, there exist cultural traditions, despite the goals and ideals of its spiritual leaders, which never reflected (nor were intended to reflect) the precepts of traditional Orthodox society. The responsibility of those born into an Orthodox milieu is to begin to distinguish these mundane traditions from the spiritual ones and to protect both their own scions and the convert population by this distinction.

In this respect, the greatest caution should be exercised, in recovering our lost traditions, in turning to modern Orthodox societies. Many true traditions have survived from the "old country," but, as we have noted, not all that is "old country"

75

is authentic. And often what is authentic must be properly understood, since most modern Orthodox societies have lost the spiritual perspective. Modern Greek society, for example, has undergone great secularization and has been very negatively influenced, in many instances, by western (and thus non-Orthodox) concepts. Until a very recent renewal of interest in patristics, even much of the academic theology in Greece had little if any relationship to the subtle mystical theology which distinguishes the Eastern Church. Priests and lay theologians were taught systematic theologies of western origin and were often encouraged to pursue "scientific" empirical views of the religious experience which almost wholly ignored the astounding richness of traditional Orthodox theology. Moreover, years of brutal enslavement of the Greek people under the Turkish yoke took a yet uncalculated toll on the magnificent Orthodox society of the late Byzantine period. Much of the richness of Orthodox tradition was lost. In such circumstances, it is not difficult to see why a frightful degeneration of Orthodox cultural traditions took place. The presence of foreign mentalities, both in the sense of a western intellectual captivity in theology and in the sense of a literal captivity politically and socially, led to the loss of many important traditions. Simultaneously, those traditions that did survive survived in circumstances that changed, at times, the essential nature of these traditions—a nature which would have been organically present in the hegemony of the holy and the mundane characteristics of pure Orthodox social structure.

In the Slavic traditions, too (especially in Russia), the traditional Orthodox societies, in which cultural traditions were made apparent in their spiritual content by the very functioning of society, have disappeared to a great extent. The majority of the Orthodox Church today labors under the yoke of communist domination. Even where the Church does speak, it is either speaking with the real threat of martyrdom (and thus in an atmosphere of immediacy lost to us in the West who are free) or through the channels of an atheistic regime. The resulting witness must be cautiously approached. And even before the horrible political conditions that now exist fell over the Orthodox of Eastern Europe, much western influence had diluted the extant holy societies. As in Greece, mystical iconography had come to be replaced with insipid western painting. Systematic western theologies, though less blatant than those in contemporary Greece, were popular in Russia. And a very romanticized view of Russian aristocratic society (perhaps prompted by the real piety of the Russian nobles at different times in history) has tended to obfuscate what many see as some very un-Orthodox threads in the fabric of Russian imperial society. Again, in such circumstances one must not be naive and cling to what one wishes were true. There are among the Slavic Orthodox, also, many traditions that should not be accepted as expressive of the Orthodox mentality and therefore are not conducive to proper spiritual growth.[1]

The weaknesses of traditional Orthodox societies were brought by emigrants to America, too. They brought with them a weakened Orthodox mentality and, in many cases, a knowledge of their own cultures in general that was not adequate. If this did not, in itself, augur well for a sound Orthodox spirituality in America, there was manifested the unfortunate process of accommodating this already diluted mentality with American culture. And the resulting mélange, however disconcerting the fact, has influenced the growth of Orthodoxy in America to no small extent. The resulting "cultural tradition" is thus spurious

(1) Parenthetically, it seems necessary here to interject several qualifying remarks regarding the foregoing paragraphs. Especially in America, where the study of the history of Orthodox countries is less developed, one is hesitant to decry any aspect of that history or of Orthodox culture, as the prejudices that might ensue would be unfair. We are attempting here to extract from these Orthodox societies their spiritual essence, and in so doing we have been cautious and critical. In this process, however, the western reader should not forget that these societies are among the greatest that man has ever developed. Whatever their shortcomings, even their secular triumphs are a witness to Orthodox history. It is from the Greeks that the West received Christianity; the Russian people civilized a vast part of Europe; Greek literary figures today continue to gain world recognition; and the Slavic countries are virtual centers of world culture even under the domination of the communists. One need only mention Dostoevsky to epitomize the blending of philosophy, literature, and culture with Orthodox spirituality, and the trenchant observations of Solzhenitsyn regarding western society suggest the continued ascendancy of the Orthodox culture and spirit.

from its very inception. This spurious "tradition" is yet another danger to which we must attend, in our attempts to regain a truly Orthodox tradition. Suffice it to say that young Greeks often cannot distinguish a prayer rope from "worry beads." And when they finally discover the difference, they hear the prayer rope described as a "rosary." They make associations with a distinct western practice with no relationship to the "Jesus Prayer," or the central practice of the hesychastic tradition, and thus create, from information resulting from ignorance of an ancient Orthodox tradition, a new and wholly improper understanding of an important part of Orthodox spirituality. The list could continue from the "Mass" through "last Rites." The point is that we do not have an authentic Orthodox cultural tradition in America and that the so-called "traditions" that we do know come to us in distorted form.

We can conclude, from our discussion, that Orthodox spirituality is transferred through a cultural medium and that the cultural traditions passed on to us from Orthodox societies can facilitate our personal spiritual growth. A mentality handed down to us from societies that modeled daily life after spiritual principles is a prerequisite for survival in a non-Orthodox society. At the same time, we must be realistic and understand that all that has been passed down from the "old country" is not Orthodox, not only because historical realities have eroded away ideal Orthodox societies, but because not every Orthodox Christian fully receives and transmits genuine tradition. Finally, we have said that in America a false Orthodox culture has emerged, based not on genuine Orthodox cultural traditions, but on distorted traditions accommodated to western models and thus not expressive of the Orthodox spirit. What, therefore, does it mean to recapture an "old country" mentality, an Orthodox cultural *paradosis,* if such does not exist in pure form? Where is the elusive cultural medium of Orthodox spirituality?

The Person and the Transpersonal Consensus. Amidst our qualifications and cautions, we have, in fact, given a clue as to the path to true Orthodox cultural traditions. All traditions of a genuine spiritual nature, it has been suggested, must relate to the spiritual life. Let us consider this first on the personal level. At the outset we noted that the adoption of "old country" habits of eating and drinking can facilitate fasting and one's religious outlook. Dressing modestly and removing oneself from the prevailing secular culture are personal requisites for fulfilling some of the most fundamental commandments of Christian life. We know by religious instruction, if not by a certain intuitive sense, what basic behaviors are necessary to separate us from society at large and to nurture our spiritual faculties. Certain church regulations regarding our moral and daily behaviors are known to us. We know how they relate to the increase of our spiritual desires and the attenuation of our less-seemly motivations. If we monitor this inward knowledge, then we have a sure way, if we are honest and seek inward guidance, of knowing what cultural traditions handed down to us lead to the expression of genuine Orthodox spirituality. This is as obvious in every case as it is in the case of incorporating into our lives dietary traditions from the "old country" that by nature fashion our eating habits to meet fasting regulations. It is as obvious as the spiritual benefit offered to those Orthodox who celebrate the Nativity of Christ on January 7 (new style), following the traditional calendar of the Church, outside of the din and the merry ring of the cash register that mark the western Christmas.

There is, above the merely personal level, a far greater criterion by which to know the genuinely Orthodox from the secular traditions of degenerating societies: that of the spiritual father, the *gerontas,* or the *staretz.* These God-bearing elders, having been raised up and joined to the mystical spirit of Orthodoxy, are perfect guides. Knowing the hearts of those Christians who appeal to them, they can give them daily guidance and rules that surely set them on the road toward spiritual enlightenment and a peaceful, pious life. These fathers, speaking with one single voice through the mouths of the Apostles and the Fathers of the Church up to our time, are, after all, the final source of our cultural traditions. Their instructions helped shape Orthodox societies. But, sadly, we live in a very barren age spiritually. Though there are still great spiritual fathers in our times, there are probably few, if any, in America. And if any exist, as most spiritual aspirants agree, they are probably silent and hidden.

Where, then, do we turn to find these transpersonal criteria for understanding what is and what is not Orthodox tradition? We turn to the only fathers we have—dead, yet living. We turn to the growing body of English-language translations of the spiritual Fathers of the Church, or, if we are fortunate enough to know or to have learned a traditional Orthodox language, to the great spiritual writings that the Church has passed on to us. And yet even this is wrought with deadly dangers. Many Fathers speak from elevated experience, and we must not aspire to their heights without first building a foundation. Then, too, we might come to a merely intellectual understanding of the great Fathers, turning arrogantly away from certain salutary traditions as being too primitive or crude for us. We can avoid these dangers only by seeing the Fathers in a spiritual light, looking for a certain inner spirit and sense of humility that true cultural traditions will also reveal to us. Thus, we must follow Orthodox traditions (it is perhaps safe to begin with fasting), seeking to avoid anything innovative, yet humbly remaining open to correction, not in this greater sense exercising our personal opinion. As our reading of the Fathers, prayer, and growth in God's grace increase, the harmony between our practices (in terms of cultural traditions) and what they yield and the spirit we find in prayer and reading will be apparent. In an automatic way, truth becomes self-validating and true Orthodox tradition becomes self-evident. But the very foundations of this spiritual ascent are the acceptance (with the caution suggested above) of the cultural traditions in which Orthodoxy has prevailed and, above all, humble submission to the consensus of the Fathers.

8

Palaioemerologitai: An Overview of the Old Calendar Orthodox Church of Greece

by

Archimandrite Chrysostomos

Western Christians and Eastern Christians following the Gregorian ("new" or civil) calendar are well aware of the Julian (or "old") calendar because of the reckoning of the Orthodox Paschal season (in all but a very few Orthodox bodies) by the old style. Most Orthodox Christians, moreover, know that some jurisdictions in the Church use the old calendar, not only to set the Paschal season, but to determine holy days throughout the year (thus falling thirteen days behind the new calendar calculation of the feasts). The phenomenon of some Orthodox Christians celebrating Christmas with the West on December 25 while others celebrate the Nativity on January 7 (December 25 by the old calendar) is not an unusual one.

But on the whole, few Orthodox or Western Christians in America know much at all about the large number of Orthodox Christians in Greece (estimated in at least the hundreds of thousands by most reliable sources, but numbered at well over a million by others) who, separated from the State Church of Greece by their use of the old calendar, constitute the Church of True Orthodox Christians of Greece (TOC) or the Ekklesia Gnesion Orthodoxon Christianon Ellados (GOCh). For a variety of reasons, which we shall consider subsequently, the witness of this Orthodox Church, ravaged at times by internal strife and subjected periodically to brutal persecution, has been silent and seldom treated objectively by those few who have written about it. Our present remarks are not intended to correct this lamentable situation, but to give a thumbnail sketch of the contemporary Old Calendarist movement in Greece.

"*Palaioemerologitai:* An Overview of the Old Calendar Orthodox Church of Greece" appeared in *Diakonia* 15:1 (1980) 32-48. Reprinted by permission.

81

The Old Calendar Change of 1924. The Old Calendarists *(Palaioemerologitai)* trace their movement to the introduction of the Gregorian calendar by the Patriarch of Constantinople in March 1924, before which time the entire Orthodox Church used the Julian calendar. The action of the Ecumenical Patriarch followed the so-called "Inter-Orthodox Conference" convened by his authority in 1923. Present at the conference were delegates from the churches of Cyprus, Greece, Serbia, and Rumania. The proposals under consideration at the meetings, *viz.,* married bishops, remarriage for widowed priests, and several other remarkable "reforms," were curiously similar to the innovations of the "Living Church" capitulation by some Russian churchmen after the communist revolution of 1917. Only the new calendar emerged as a definite decision of the conference.

The Patriarchate's decision was followed by the adoption of the Gregorian calendar shortly afterwards by the churches of Alexandria, Antioch, Cyprus, Greece, Poland, and Rumania (though about one million of the Rumanian faithful, mostly in Moldavia, still adhere to the Julian calendar). The churches of Finland and Bulgaria have also since accepted the new calendar. However, the churches of Jerusalem, Russia, and Serbia, along with the Old Calendarists in Greece, refused to adopt the Gregorian calendar. And, though they did not rupture communion with the Ecumenical Patriarch or the State Church of Greece, as did the Old Calendaritsts in Greece proper, almost all of the monasteries of the Holy Mountain of Athos refused to follow the new calendar. (The Holy Mountain remains to this day on the old calendar.) Thus, if one relies on the more reasonable estimates of the Orthodox population of the Soviet Union, the Eastern Orthodox Church remains, despite the Constantinopolitan reform, significantly old calendarist.

Reaction to the New Calendar in Greece. Many of the faithful and clergy in Greece were quick to react to the acceptance of the new calendar by the State Church of Greece in 1924 by disavowing the change. Certainly the most eminent churchman to separate himself from the State Church was the Metropolitan

Bishop of Florina (in northern Greece), referred to by contemporary Old Calendarists as Chrysostomos of "Blessed Memory." It was his basic argument (and that of the Old Calendarists in general) that the church calendar and, of course, the dating of Pascha (Easter) were established by catholic councils of the Church and that no local church (and certainly not the Patriarchate itself), but only the entire Church could make a decision regarding these issues.

Moreover, he was undoubtedly right in questioning the entire context in which the calendar change was effected; amidst the discussion of radical changes that were contradictory to centuries of Orthodox practice and tradition. The issue, then, was not primarily one of dates and calendars, as polemical writers with little insight into the matter have often suggested, but one of the very order of the Church, of the Church's very polity. It was Bishop Chrysostomos' moderate attitude, not a senseless, conservative adherence to a calendar, that initially motivated him in his rupture with the State Church. He and those who followed him questioned the rashness of the issue raised by the patriarchal conference of 1923, as well as the precipitance of overturning the church calendar handed down from the apostolic Church, preferred (as evidenced by repeated conciliar decrees) over the western calendar through the centuries by the Church, and symbolic of the hegemony of the national Orthodox churches.

At the same time, the Old Calendarists were extremely wary of the rupture of external liturgical unity in the Orthodox world by the introduction of the new calendar, which heralded the curious manifestation, today, of various Orthodox churches celebrating church feasts thirteen days apart. This concern belies the notion that Metropolitan Chrysostomos and the faithful with him rushed headlong into schism and were unsympathetic to the sacrosanctity of the unity of the Church of Greece. They were, indeed, acutely aware of the sacrosanctity of that unity throughout the Church, not only internally and mystically, but manifestly and externally. Furthermore, Bishop Chrysostomos at first personally characterized the old calendar struggle as a temporary protest, as an attempt to bring the Greek Church to its senses and to attenuate its own rash schism, in his view, with the rest of the old calendar Orthodox world. His protest was, indeed, a mature theological warning: a strong plea for moderation in the entry of the Church of Greece into the modern era, a desire for the return of churchmen to the cautious, slow, natural process by which true tradition, in Orthodox history, has triumphed over the whims, excesses and fancies of the prevailing *Zeitgeist* and through which, by the same token, necessary change has been made manifest.

One senses in the efforts of the first ranks of the Greek Old Calendarists not fanaticism or conservatism for the sake of conservatism, but an understanding of the true nature of a church council, of the *phronema* or mind of the Church as it is unveiled in history—not by sudden innovations and renewals and reforms born of accommodation to some "historical" or "social" truth, but by sound spiritual judgments developed over years and naturally accepted in due process by the body of the faithful in spiritual consensus.

And if their protest came to be permanent, and not temporary, as intended, this might be an indictment of the incautious way that we today speak of change in the Church, not evidence of blind conservatism or fanaticism among the early Old Calendarist Greeks. Along with the late Archimandrite Justin Popovich, that great Serbian father whose trenchant observations have not yet fully had their impact on our reactions as Orthodox to the contingencies and presumed realities of modernity, Metropolitan Chrysostomos and his followers present to us an authentic witness of the true Orthodox view of tradition. We should not ignore this witness because of our polemic misunderstanding of its intent. How especially true this is as Orthodox face the prospect of a pan-Orthodox conference (or would-be ecumenical synod) which intends to consider the very innovative and revolutionary issues to which the Greek Old Calendarists originally reacted.

Persecution and Permanence. If the original Old Calendarist protest was not a fanatic one aimed at schism and mere conservatism, the unintended permanence of its witness was to see the unfortunate and tragic emergence of these abuses in some circles (though in lesser degree than polemical observers would have it). But this emergence must be seen in the light of the very intransigence of the innovation and modernity to which the Old Calendarists protested and the shameful persecution that befell them under the aegis of the Greek civil and ecclesiastical authorities. One is disinclined, more out of embarrassment at the actions of the Greek authorities than out of a hesitancy to evoke needless visions of horrendous maltreatment among the Old Calendarist victims, to chronicle the brutality experienced by the *Palaioemerologitai*. Suffice it to say that, merely because of their refusal to follow the State Church and its calendar reform, countless Old Calendarists were imprisoned for their beliefs.

Hardly a single Old Calendarist community in modern Greece is without a clergyman or a member of the faithful who has a story of such persecution. The memory of priests being shaved, stripped of their clerical garb, and thrown into jails is, for most Old Calendarists, a vivid one. In addition to periodic molestations of the clergy and the faithful up to very recent time, it has been almost impossible, right up to the present, for Old Calendarist clergy to gain admission to theological seminaries or to the theological faculties of the state universities. Much to the shame of the Greek government, many Old Calendarist clergy still find it difficult to travel outside Greece. From a purely psychological standpoint, the appearance of fanaticism (or conservative resistance to any dialogue with the State Church) among some members of the Old Calendarist movement was, therefore, certainly inevitable in view of the brutal policies of the State Church toward the Old Calendarists. If their movement was originally in the form of a temporary protest, mistreatment drove them to an intractable position of permanent protest against the new calendar church. And while the State Church of Greece should not be wholly condemned for what was at times overreaction and probably policy carelessly enacted, it must bear some responsibility for the crystal-lization of opposition that made the Old Calendarist movement what it became.

One would be remiss in failing to note, too, the role that the intense feelings of the Old Calendarists as "guardians of the faith" came to play in contributing to the permanence of their witness. The movement, from its very inception, felt a holy commission to preserve Orthodox tradition in the face of mod-ernism. As such, it was perhaps destined to be more than an ephemeral protest movement. Evidential (if not a validation) of this destiny was an event to which the Old Calendarists hearken as a clear, divine herald of their cause: the miraculous mani-festation in a small Greek village of a Byzantine cross in the evening sky, over a small church dedicated to St. John the Theologian, on the eve of the Feast of the Exaltation of the Holy Cross in 1925. If there was any doubt among the faithful (many of whom, along with the officials assigned to control the gathering, had witnessed and reported this amazing manifes-tation) regarding the singular witness of the Old Calendar Church, the events of the evening of September 13, 1925 (old style) certainly dismissed that doubt.

It seemed obvious to all very shortly that the Old Calendarist movement had now become a divine mission—no longer a pro-test, but an authentic, divinely appointed witness of "True" Orthodoxy in Greece. It seemed equally obvious that the au-thority claimed by the State Church, which had so brutally opposed the Old Calendarist protest, had passed on to the Church of True Orthodox Christians of Greece.[1]

The Old Calendarists in Contemporary Greece. Both the permanence of the Old Calendarist movement and its struggle with internal problems, born out of years of persecution, are witnessed by the existence of three separate synods of Old Cal-

(1) We should incidentally remark that, in recognition of the significance of this event, the synod of Old Calendarist bishops under the presidency of Metropolitan Kallistos of Corinth has appointed a feast day in commemoration of the appearance of the Holy Cross in 1925.

endarists in modern Greece, all calling themselves the Church of True Orthodox Christians of Greece and claiming to continue the unbroken witness of the ancient Greek Church. The first (and smallest) of these is the synod of Archbishop Andreas (of Athens and All Greece), whose bishops, clergy, and faithful honor particularly the memory of Bishop Matthew, one of the earliest Old Calendarist prelates. (Hence, they are often called "Matthewites.") Bishop Matthew's consecration of hierarchs to succeed him under canonically questionable circumstances has left the taint of irregularity on the image of this group, though recently the canonical issue was resolved by the intervention of bishops of the Russian Church Abroad in validating the episcopal orders of the "Matthewites."

More seriously damaging, however (from the standpoint of its appeal to a more general Orthodox community), have been the extreme claims to exclusivity coming from the synod of Archbishop Andreas. His synod and clergy have come to believe themselves the only genuine Orthodox Christians in the world, eschewing not only new calendarists and other Greek Old Calendarists, but the synod of bishops of the Russian Orthodox Church Abroad (itself, of course, adhering to the Julian calendar), to which they turned, paradoxically enough, for the normalization of their canonical status. Their extreme fanaticism and exclusivity, doubtless partly stemming from extremist reactions to harsh persecution from a church which they had every cause to consider un-Orthodox and un-Christian in terms of gut emotional responses, have made their witness in Greece and in world Orthodoxy a largely unconscionable one.

The jurisdiction of Archbishop Auxentios (also holding the title of Athens and All Greece) constitutes a second group of Old Calendarists. Until the very recent reform of his synod by the bishops of a third Old Calendarist group, which we shall consider shortly, Archbishop Auxentios led the majority of the Old Calendarists of Greece (along with synodal exarchates in Australia, Canada, various locales in Central Europe, and the US). These Old Calendarists, fearful of the canonical anomalies that marked the "Matthewites," had very early on in the movement turned to the Russian Church Abroad to establish a Greek hierarchy after the death of Metropolitan Chrysostomos. They trace their original hierarchy, therefore, to a church body external to the Greek Old Calendarist movement and thus naturally maintained a less exclusivistic outlook toward the Orthodox world in general (while enjoying, in their association with the Russians, full canonicity). Moreover, the enthusiastic fraternal interest of some bishops of the Russian Church Abroad (Archbishop Leonty of Chile, Archbishop John of San Francisco, Archbishop Seraphim of Chicago, Bishop Sava of Edmonton and, of course, Metropolitan Philaret, among others) kept this external contact viable.

For about a decade, however, Archbishop Auxentios and his synod have moved toward a position more and more similar to that of the "Matthewites." This resulted in a decision by the synod, some years ago, to declare the mysteries (sacraments) of the State Church of Greece without grace and therefore invalid. Many clergy, contending that decisions of the magnitude of declaring an Orthodox body outside grace can be settled only by a universal council of the Church (in the irony of the *lex talionis*, thereby using the reasoning of the original Old Calendarist resistance to the calendar reform against the Old Calendarists themselves), objected to this immoderate declaration. The exarch of the synod in the United States, Bishop Petros of Astoria, refused to sign the synod's decree and became a kind of ecclesiastical persona non grata, remaining, until very recently, independent of any Old Calendarist group and of the Russian Orthodox Church Abroad (two of whose bishops had consecrated him to the episcopacy). Respected by many for his judicious and moderate stand, Bishop Petros became the tragic victim of the Auxentian synod's move toward some of the more fanatical elements of the Old Calendarist movement. More importantly, this disputed decision led to further rash actions and decisions that alienated the Russian synod, finally culminating in a rupture of relations with the Russian bishops by Auxentios and his synod.

The more moderate and concerned voices in Archbishop

Auxentios' synod urged reform and the repair of relations with the Russian Church Abroad. Their voices were finally heeded when, all else having failed, two of Archbishop Auxentios' hierarchs, Bishop Kallistos (Metropolitan of Corinth) and Bishop Antonios (Metropolitan of Attica), consecrated to the episcopacy eight well-educated, respected churchmen, all of whom, along with the two consecrating hierarchs, wished to right the abuses that had multiplied under Archbishop Auxentios. When Archbishop Auxentios refused to accept the actions of his two hierarchs and the legitimacy of the new bishops, a schism ensued and a new synod, the third group of Old Calendarists, was formed under Metropolitan Kallistos. Archbishop Auxentios was deposed, but he and his followers, having lost great numbers of the faithful to the reforms of the new synod, have nonetheless refused to relinquish their claims to the Church, thus maintaining an adherence of their own.

The Third Group. This third group of Old Calendarists has struck an image that makes it (already a very large Old Calendarist church in Greece) perhaps destined to bring a unity long hoped for to the Greek traditionalists. The president of the synod (an archbishop has yet to be elected by a clergy-laity vote), Metropolitan Kallistos, came to the Auxentian group, before the recent reform, from the "Matthewites." His resistance to their condemnation of the Russian Synod had prompted the move. He thus forms a bridge between the ranks of the more excessive Old Calendarists and more moderate voices. And his reputation and distinction as a man of spiritual attainment comparable to that of the ancient Fathers, combined with a fierce loyalty to traditional Orthodoxy that earned him imprisonment and great personal humility, bring a person of great charisma and popular appeal to the forefront. The first new bishop consecrated, Metropolitan Cyprian of Oropos, is another outstanding figure. As Bishop-Abbot and spiritual father of the Holy Monastery of Sts. Cyprian and Justina (in Fili, just outside Athens), an active community of young and exceptionally well-educated monks, his spiritual guidance will undoubtedly be felt in the future leadership of the Church.[2] Being a spiritual son of the renowned elder Archimandrite Philotheos (Zervakos) and having close relationships with the more traditionalist circles in the State Church of Greece (he and his monks left the State Church a number of years ago, out of concern for what they saw as its unwise accommodation to modernity, and joined the Old Calendar Church), Metropolitan Cyprian is a natural link between the new and old calendar Greek churches and can no doubt do much to bring about more fruitful relations between them. Very concerted efforts have been expended, also, to re-establish close ties with the Russian synod, to improve the education of the clergy (something sorely neglected by the Old Calendarists in general for decades) and to achieve unity in the Old Calendarist movement both in Greece and abroad.

The World Witness of the Old Calendarists. In the early years of the Old Calendarist movement, the realities of dealing with survival in Greece against the odds of persecution and growing factionalism in the ranks precluded much association with world Orthodoxy. There was, of course, the normal intercourse between the Greek Old Calendarists and the Russian Church Abroad, connected with the latter's establishment of a hierarchy for the Greeks, but these relationships did not extend much beyond the task of that establishment and certainly did not reach out to other Orthodox bodies. Old Calendarist Greeks in diaspora, however, did interact at times with other Orthodox groups, most especially in the jurisdictional "melting pot" of America. Thus, for a brief period two decades ago, a Greek faction, under the leadership of Bishop (then Archimandrite) Petros of Astoria *(supra)* even came under the omophorion of Metropolitan Leonty (Turkevich), then chief prelate of the so-called Russian Metropolia (now the Orthodox Church in America). But other than these associations, until reasonably recently the Old Calendarists have been very much a movement unto themselves.[3]

(2) Already, one of his monks has been elevated to the episcopacy.

(3) It should be noted here that the "Matthewites" have never had more than a negligible following outside Greece.

The efforts of the new synod of Metropolitan Kallistos to reestablish a close relationship and to renew intercommunion between his group and the Russian Church Abroad indicate a serious move toward participation in world Orthodoxy, or at least a real sensibility to a broader Orthodox witness. This indication is supported by the bonds between the new synod and the Old Calendar Orthodox Church of Rumania. Metropolitan Cyprian of Oropos has personally visited Rumania and was instrumental in setting the stage that finally led to the official mutual recognition of the Old Calendarists of these two countries as sister churches in late 1979. His monastery, through the skills of his multilingual monks, handles relations with the Rumanian hierarchy.

The Old Calendarist exarchates outside Greece have, as of this writing, for the most part been hard pressed to react to the events of Greece that led to the deposition of Archibishop Auxentios. While Bishop Petros of Astoria has petitioned to join his jurisdiction to Metropolitan Kallistos' synod, Metropolitan Akakios, Auxentian exarch in Canada, has not made a decision regarding his adherence to or disavowal of the new synod. The Old Calendarist churches in Central Europe and Australia are similarly undecided. However, the few Auxentian Old Calendarist Greek parishes in the United States (including communities in Illinois, Massachusetts, Michigan, New York, and a small monastic dependency under Metropolitan Cyprian of Oropos located in Ohio) have all joined themselves to the new synod of Metropolitan Kallistos. It was partly their vociferous protests to the appointment of Bishop Paisios of Astoria as exarch for the Americas by Archbishop Auxentios that led to the deposition of the archbishop. The US parishes had refused to accept the newly appointed bishop on the grounds that Bishop Petros of Astoria had never been actually deposed and that the new exarch, Paisios, was an unacceptable candidate for the episcopacy. Bishop Paisios was subsequently convicted of very serious charges by the new synod and defrocked, thus seriously limiting his claims to leadership in the US Old Calendarist communities.

91

Continued Misunderstanding and Prejudice. If recent developments in the Old Calendarist movement in Greece are harbingers of future unity and solidarity in the movement, the prospects for a better understanding and treatment of Old Calendarists by the new calendar Greek churches do not augur of success. Despite dominant moderate elements among the traditionalists, the new calendar ecclesiastical press invariably holds up the actions of the fanatical Old Calendarists as typical of the movement. The creation of a new synod under Metropolitan Kallistos was met with few positive comments and seemed to trigger a senseless barrage of printed invective against the Old Calendarists as factions of warring illiterates not only inclined toward, but desirous, in their pugnacious spirit, of division and schism.

One is tempted to see very much the same overreaction, on the part of the State Church, that originally alienated the Old Calendarists and contributed to their intransigence. And certainly any objective observer would find it tragically ironic that, having seen to it that the Old Calendarists were denied access to the centers of academic theological learning in Greece, the State Church would convict them of illiteracy.[4]

Equally disturbing in the State Church press treatment of the Old Calendarists is the persistent accusation of uncanonicity against them. Though the original bishops consecrated by Bishop Matthew certainly invited, to some extent, reservations about their canonical status, the correction of this irregularity by the Russian Orthodox Church Abroad (the canonicity of which has been recognized by the State Church of Greece) certainly must be acknowledged. Moreover, all other Greek Old Calendarists received their orders from the Russian Church Abroad initially. The only accurate statement that can be made

(4) In actual fact, of course, many Old Calendarists maintained, throughout the years of persecution, both an academic knowledge of theology and the more important theological learning naturally consistent with their tremendous emphasis on the preservation of monastic life and institutions. The synod under Metropolitan Kallistos, furthermore, plans to establish a theological seminary under the direct auspices of the Old Calendar Church itself—which is evidence of the availability of competent teachers and theologians among their ranks.

92

of them, therefore, is that they are separated from the State Church of Greece. Their canonicity is a matter of fact.

It is in America, however, that misunderstanding of and prejudice against the Old Calendarists have become particularly ugly. In Greece, where the beards, long hair, and black robes of the clergy are common to new and Old Calendarists, the Old Calendarist clergymen are not visibly distinct. But in America, where most new calendarist Greeks (under the Ecumenical Patriarchate) have abandoned traditional clerical dress for the western style, the traditionally garbed Old Calendarists are at once distinct and, at times, a source of discomfort to those new calendarists who have misgivings about the more modern ecclesiastical usage in America.[5] The Old Calendarist traditionalism also stresses the strictness of the fasting periods, the importance of monastic ideals as a foundation for authentic Orthodoxy (the majority of monastic communities in Greece, indeed, belong to the Old Calendarists), and the celebration of a more or less complete cycle of services even at the parish level. These practices have challenged the laxity of the new calendar Church, which is attempting to come to grips with the non-Orthodox society around it (and the toll that American society is taking on its young) by a redefinition of practice in these areas (e.g., relaxed fasting rules, the virtual disappearance of some services, and shortened Liturgies).

Further Conflicts. The Old Calendarist resistance to the new calendar role in the ecumenical movement—the Old Calendarists prescribing a far more limited, careful, and exclusivistic approach to heterodox bodies (emphasizing that ecumenicity cannot prove fruitful if it compromises Orthodox tradition)—has also provided grounds for conflict. This confrontation has left the traditionalists, a mere handful in the United States (but distinct and visible), at the mercy of the polemical voices in the larger new calendar Church (with over a million adherents).

(5) The traditionalists argue that clerical dress is not a matter of personal taste, but of historical tradition and spiritual importance, thus exacerbating the discomfort of the new calendarists who are sensitive to the issue.

That mercy has not been seemly, much to the misfortune of all involved.

The most common maltreatment by polemicists in the new calendar Church in America has been the shameful tendency to link legitimate Greek Old Calendarists to the various self-proclaimed or deposed "prelates" (some actually using the Julian calendar, but not part of the Old Calendarist movement) who have fled Greece to avail themselves of the religious freedom afforded by America and to avoid the sure disapproval they would face in Greece. This "guilt" by deceptive association is, of course, an egregious injustice. There have been attempts, too, to hold up those Old Calendarist churchmen who are obviously poor pastors (a small population lamentably known to any jurisdiction) not as the exception, but as the norm. Finally, there have even been instances of willingness to engage in the open molestation of Old Calendarists. Thus, the incredible story of a small Old Calendarist community in a rural Ohio village, where Greek Orthodoxy was unknown to local authorities, being asked (despite its legal incorporation as a religious organization) to disprove its links with any Satanic cultic activity. While the status of the community was clearly established by communiqués of outrage from Greece and protests from clergy and lay leaders, an antagonist had actually offered the services of a new calendar clergyman to the authorities to verify that the community was, indeed, not Orthodox. One would hope that responsible churchmen in the new calendar Church (and there are, to be sure, many who decry the more polemical voices) would speak out openly to end this mistreatment of the Old Calendarists and that the traditionalists, in turn, would moderate their rhetorical opposition to the new calendar American Church.

The Greek Old Calendarists in the United States have also come under attack from an unlikely party: Greek Old Calendarists under indigenous American jurisdictions. Many of these Old Calendarists were members of the new calendar Greek Church in the US who, finding the modernistic trends in that jurisdiction incompatible with their traditionalist bent, broke away and placed themselves under other national jurisdictions.

94

The hesitancy to seek shelter under the wings of the Old Calendarist Church of Greece stemmed from the realities to which we have alluded above: the precipitous movement of the Greek Church toward unconscionable exclusivity and the consequent independent (and thus canonically uncertain) stance of its exarchate in the United States. Over the years, however, certain among these Old Calendarists have ironically developed the exclusivistic notion that only they have preserved true Orthodoxy and that other Orthodox may well be simply heretics. The recent move of other Old Calendarist Greek parishes in the US to the moderate synod of Metropolitan Kallistos, then, has not only failed at winning their approval, but has elicited disapproval in far from uncertain terms. Their attacks against the Old Calendarists bound to the Church in Greece have caused dismay and shock among those who seek for Old Calendarist unity in America. A very unfruitful, counterproductive clash with these groups in non-Greek jurisdictions (often in an atmosphere marked by animosity, near character assassination, and pathological commitment to personal figures) can only promise more abuse for the less-organized and persecuted parishes under the jurisdiction of the Church of Greece.

The Future of the Old Calendarists: Weaknesses and Strengths. As a result of years of alienation from other Orthodox bodies, persecution, and difficulty in maintaining an educated clergy, the Greek Old Calendarists today are encountering prodigious and seemingly insurmountable problems. While, among the more learned and responsible clergy, the Old Calendarists have manifested a healthy, patristic wariness of learning for the mere sake of learning and of the position that academic theological preparation alone, without corresponding spiritual practice and attainment, is sufficient for priestly ordination, often this wisdom, in less-educated circles, has deteriorated into anti-intellectualism. The presence of these anti-intellectual elements, with all of the foibles consequent to such an outlook, contributes to a rather poor self-presentation, at times, of the Old Calendarist witness.

This poor self-presentation, in turn, further serves to alienate the entire movement, including the moderate voices. Largely as a result of this anti-intellectual spirit, advocates of a lamentably exclusivistic and unconscionable fanaticism find receptive ears for their claims to sole possession of a genuine Orthodoxy (often, unbelievably enough, characterizing this singular possession as an ethnic privilege!) and their ludicrous approach to other Orthodox according to the traditional protocol for the treatment of heretics.[6] What this often means is that educated and moderate voices in the Church cannot speak in a representative manner and, in expressing their moderation, often suffer the condemnation of these less-enlightened circles. The prospects of Old Calendarist unity, then, are bleak. Moreover, if the moderate group of Old Calendarists who seek unity were to accomplish a consolidation of all Old Calendarist groups, the pluralism of that united body (with a range of ideas from the most extreme to the most considered) would no doubt very shortly evoke a new schism. It is, probably and realistically, only in the fairly far distant future that Old Calendarist unity can be achieved.

The weaknesses of the Church in the United States are far less ominous than those of the Church in Greece, but they nonetheless reflect problems that defy immediate resolution. Being outside the mainstream of Orthodox life in America because of their small numbers and the sorrowful resistance they meet from the new calendarist Greek Church, the Old Calendarists confront tremendous perplexities in expanding their witness. The cooperation and mutual aid that have helped other small jurisdictions in America survive are denied the Old Calendarists in America. The few parishes in the United States are also poorly organized and their association with one another is not formally defined. Lacking any formal diocesan structure or clerical administration, what little direction of the Church that

---

(6) It should be noted that these more fanatic elements have lost completely a theological understanding of heresy and, therefore, apply the term quite injudiciously and incorrectly from the theological point of view.

exists has fallen, unfortunately, into the hands of laymen, and serious spiritual guidance is almost wholly absent.

Also, some fanaticism has surfaced in the US parishes, and it has been actualized in extremely immature and sometimes insolent behavior toward the new calendarist Greeks. This counterproductive trend, however, is being protested by some able and vocal clergymen who decry its effects and who desire a proper and objective presentation of the Old Calendarist witness. Most frightful, however, has been the failure of the Old Calendarists in the United States to recognize the indisputable fact that other jurisdictions in the diaspora have come to face: the future of the Church is dependent not on its temporary and extraordinary witness to an immigrant population (which, in the case of native Greeks, is very rapidly declining) but on its ability to maintain a witness among the ''Americanized'' children of these immigrants and among converts. A good many lay leaders (in an ironic denial of the very principles which make the Orthodox Church multilingual and multinational) identify immigrants, recently arrived from Greece, as somehow more authentically Orthodox than the indigenous Greek-American population. This naive and romantic notion notwithstanding, the future of the Old Calendarist Church in America stands or falls on its ability to deal with this last weakness.

Important Contribution. If the Old Calendarists can succeed in overcoming the terrible problems that face them, they have a singularly important contribution to make to world orthodoxy. This is their most important strength. As the ranks of educated Old Calendarists grow and their movement is correctly, moderately, and intelligently presented, there is no doubt that the movement's self-characterization as the authentic witness of the Orthodoxy of Greece, the guardian of an unbroken ''golden thread'' of Holy Tradition woven throughout the fabric of Greek ecclesiastical life and history, will be taken more and more seriously. In an Orthodox world moving perilously close to total accommodation to the passing whims and fancies of the modern world, arguing that contemporary exigencies disallow traditional

Orthodox life, the Old Calendarist witness can be a soberingly striking one. The more moderate Old Calendarists have, in fact, adjusted to modern life while, at the same time, maintaining the very externals of the Orthodox *ethos* (with traditional clerical dress, the full liturgical life, adherence to the fasting regulations of the Church, etc.). Their external adjustment facilitates a normal internal reception of Orthodoxy, not as a mere belief system and a collection of authentic and truthful dogmatic formulations, but as a style and manner of approaching life so complete and expansive that it touches on our eating habits, posture, manner of dress, and even our cognitive structure. As an answer to the tragic (yet at times certainly sincere and honest) struggle of the new calendar Church to accommodate Orthodoxy to modernity, the Old Calendarists, at least in their better representatives, can help formulate a *Weltansicht* by which modernity is accommodated to Orthodoxy.

Perhaps the greatest strength of the Old Calendar Greek Church is the potential addition of its voice to the voices of other traditionalist jurisdictions in confronting world ecumenism with an Orthodox response that deserves to be heard. The Old Calendarists sincerely believe that they have preserved the true Christian faith, passed down in Holy Tradition without essential change. They and these other traditionalists (e.g., the followers of Archimandrite Justin of Serbia, the Russian Orthodox Church Abroad, and the Old Calendar Rumanian Church) believe that it is their task to share a Christianity which has known no reformation, no counter-reformation, and none of the scholastic rigidity of western theology. Their ecumenical outlook is one of sharing an established truth and not one of discovering, through dialogue, the lost church of Christian institutional unity. The traditionalist Orthodox have much to offer, then, in terms of seeing Christianity through the eyes of those who have never thought of themselves as outside the vibrant, living, apostolic truth which shook the foundations of ancient Rome and which has power even in the atomic age.

The richness of this experience is not to be had from those modernist Orthodox who have made it their task to rediscover, revitalize, and redefine the Church vis-à-vis the supposed realities of modern life and the goal of unifying with other Christians. However useful the role of these latter Orthodox in the ecumenical movement, their views are not the only Orthodox ones. A mature ecumenicity must be willing to hear the traditionalist voice, learn from the outlook and spirit of the Old Calendarists, and have the strength, sincerity, and grace to tolerate them for what they are and for what they claim to be. The price of suffering, persecution, and misunderstanding has been paid. The Old Calendarists are now due the reward of objective and sympathetic attention.

9
Orthodoxy and the Cults
by
ARCHIMANDRITE CHRYSOSTOMOS

In the wake of an alarming increase in the number and activities of cults in the Americas and in Eastern and Western Europe, there is ever-greater attention by theologians, sociologists, psychologists, and anthropologists to the question of what constitutes a valid religion and what constitutes a cult. The glut of articles on this subject in the popular press, in church periodicals, and in some academic journals attests to its consideration as an important social issue. On the whole, these responses have been essentially pragmatic and not theological; that is, writers have attempted to guide individuals toward more established religious groups, away from groups overly dependent on the personal charisma of a cult leader, and to offer guidelines that distinguish the so-called "self-styled" religions from the established religious bodies. This pragmatic approach emphasizes, for example, that one should seek out a Christian group (and our concern here is solely with Christian groups) that shares most of the fundamental tenets of the "mainline" churches: the preeminent authority of Scripture, the divinity of Christ, a catholic view of the Church (as a universal body open to all, not just to a small fragment of humanity), and dependency on the grace of God rather than the efficacy of mere human action. In effect, one distinguishes the cult from the "valid" believing body by social comparison: the "existing" with the "would be," the "traditional" with the "innovative." All of the rejoinders, qualifiers, exceptions, and limitations aside, from a pragmatic viewpoint these characteristics are the few that really offer the proverbial "handle" on the subject. They are probably distinguishing criteria which Christians in general, from Orthodox to Reformed, can readily identify and validate.

But what if these criteria are theological and not pragmatic? Dependence on God's grace over the efforts of man, for example, is a supposition acceptable to Orthodox. But when this supposition becomes theological (i.e., doctrinaire, in our present usage) and asserts the formula of the Reformation *sola gratia,* then where is the Orthodox Christian? Not confined by such a precise formula, he might stand condemned as a member of a cult, in the most pejorative sense of that word. And the unfortunate fact is that these distinguishing characteristics have, indeed, been made theological. More than two decades ago, Kurt Hutten, in his *Die Glaubenswelt des Sektierers,*[1] one of the most complete Protestant treatments of cultism, set out to characterize the cult and, in so doing, interpreted the very characteristics to which we have alluded above specifically and in detail vis-à-vis Reformed theology.[2] Our concern, then, is that if the definition of a cultist group takes on a wholly doctrinaire meaning, the implications, especially for Orthodox, are not encouraging.

First, needless to say, no single theological tradition should be established as the comparative "other" by which the cult is distinguished. If this were so, moreover, the Orthodox, with a venerable and ancient tradition surpassed by no other Christian church, should constitute the valid criterion of judgment. Secondly, whereas churches growing out of the Reformed tradition have an influential and populous representation in the Americas and in Western Europe, Orthodox populations in these areas are less evident. It is, in such a circumstance, easy to confuse Reformation theological formulas as the "mainstream" ones and to relegate the Orthodox position, by inference, to a cultist level. Finally, it has been noted elsewhere[3] that Orthodox, especially in the Americas, are struggling to establish a firm sub-

"Orthodoxy and the Cults" appeared in the *Greek Orthodox Theological Review* 25:1 (1980) 37-48. Reprinted by permission. The author wishes to express a profound debt of gratitude to the Rev. Dr. Achilles Siagris, pastor of St. Nicholas Greek Orthodox Church, Lorain, Ohio, for his unique scholarly insight and his helpful critique of many of the thoughts and ideas expressed in this chapter.

(1) Kurt Hutten, *Die Glaubenswelt des Sektierers* (Hamburg, 1957).

(2) Our admittedly broad use of the term "Reformed" in this article refers to tenets commonly held in common by the principal churches originating in the Reformation, not only to the specific post-Lutheran reformed groups (of Calvin, Zwingli, etc.) which at times champion the term. It is a usage noted in Hutten, note 1.

(3) See Archimandrite Chrysostomos and Hierodeacon Akakios, "Some Thoughtful Comments on Orthodox Meditation," printed above as chapter 6 of the present volume.

structure for spiritual self-knowledge. In such a delicate stage of development, Orthodox are too easily apt to apologize for their ostensible irregularities in the face of a western theological system or lexicon largely inappropriate and inapplicable to them. There arises the occasion, then, for Orthodox, confronted with Reformation theological definitions of the cult, either to fail to grasp the significance of their own witness (out of fear of conviction as a cult), or subtly and unwittingly to distort their own self-presentation in order to meet a demand characteristic of the definition of validity offered from outside their own tradition. For these reasons, we think it timely to confront Hutten's formulation of the characteristics of the cult with an Orthodox response. In this way we might "de-Reformationize," so to speak, these characteristics and provide an Orthodox insight into the question of cults versus valid religions that does not compromise our own religious validity. Such a response is crucial and long overdue.[4]

Hutten identifies four major characteristics of the cults. The first of these he calls the phenomenon of a "Bible in the left hand." Alluding to the ordination of an individual into the Swedenborgian ministry while holding a Bible in his right hand and one of Swedenborg's books in his left, Hutten quite rightly suggests that "Christian" cults, in an attempt to support their particular nonbiblical doctrines, must supplement scriptural authority (to which they usually subjugate themselves as "Christians") with extrascriptural sources for those doctrines. These sources are often called reinterpretive texts, which suppose either a new revelation or knowledge from hitherto undiscovered revelatory writings. We tend to agree with Professor Hutten that cult activists do seem to gravitate towards nonscriptural sources of authority. It is a historically verified characteristic to be observed equally dominant in movements so divergent as Mormonism and nineteenth-century pietistic humanism. And its

(4) We might note here, too, that recent dialogues between Greek Orthodox and Evangelical Christians (see Stanley Harakas, "New Directions in Orthodox Ecumenism," *Greek Orthodox Theological Review* 24 [1979] 76-77) make an Orthodox response to these earlier Protestant formulations crucial and timely.

most frightening danger is that extrascriptural authorities, often modeled after scriptural language and using scriptural imagery, often in scriptural style, and just as often treated with the same veneration as Scripture, attract to themselves, by association, the virtual authority of the Bible itself. An otherwise Bible-oriented Christian attributes to these extrascriptural sources, in a subtle, perhaps unrecognized, manner, the authoritative "context" and aura of recognized inspired texts.

The first characteristic of the cult is not compromising of the Orthodox self-presentation if it remains fundamentally functional in application. But when one begins to voice the Reformation motto *sola scriptura* theologically, contending that there is no source of authority other than the Bible, then a statement unacceptable to the Orthodox Christian is made. Indeed, the Orthodox Church exalts the authority of Scripture, but at the same time it recognizes and exalts the authoritative and inspired nature of the unwritten apostolic tradition, the seven holy ecumenical councils, and the writings of the Church Fathers. For indeed, the Holy Spirit did not cease inspiring Christians subsequent to the completion of the accepted canon of Scripture. And never has the Eastern Church lost the spirit of the Evangelist Philip when he set forth to "guide" (Acts 8:31) the Ethiopian queen's eunuch in understanding Scripture. The Eastern Orthodox Church triumphs the hermeneutic thrust of patristic writings and their integral involvement in the very transferal of the meaning of Scripture to the faithful. This living hermeneutic tradition cannot be separated from Scripture any more than water can be separated from its hydraulic powers; for it is an essential part of the Scripture's authority, witnessed by the fact that (however discomforting this may be to those who suppose the Bible to have dropped as if by divine intervention into the very hands of the believers of the early Church) Scripture is itself the product of the authority of tradition, since the canon of Scripture is the product of synodical authority, the external, formal expression of church tradition.

Theologically, therefore, the Orthodox Church neither denies the authority of Scripture *nor* limits the source of spiritual authority to the Bible itself. Authority was, in the early Church (and the Orthodox Church claims to express the spirit of that Church *in toto*), a far more metaphysical concept than we today imagine, something not subject to dissection and precise definition. St. Athanasios saw authority in the "skopon tes pisteos,"[5] an expansive notion to which a formula like *sola scriptura* cannot be reasonably contrasted. The latter expression is too definitive, too constrictive, and too unexpressive of the ineffable authority of truth as the early Church viewed it. Moreover, the early Church, in the more definitive sense, never considered all of Scripture to be contained in what came to be the biblical canon. St. Basil the Great, in fact, as one Orthodox theologian notes, contended that revelation "was not all delivered in written form."[6] Scripture is a body of knowledge passed down in the Church in many forms. The holy ecumenical synods, the Fathers of the Church, their inspired writings, and the corpus of tradition that constitutes Orthodoxy are, in many ways, Scripture itself, completing and witnessing, yet never supplanting or contradicting, the written biblical canon.

What one must emphasize in confronting Hutten's objection to extrabiblical authority in the Church is his very doctrinaire notion of what constitutes Scripture. To be sure, one must fear any amplification of the biblical canon that detracts from or alters its truth. But such a fear certainly does not apply to the Orthodox Church and its venerable patristic literature, sharing, as it does, the historical source of written Scripture and expressing, in an unbroken patristic consensus, the very existential essence of that scriptural authority. It would seem that Protestants, in calling themselves Lutherans or Calvinists, would be better advised, despite their adherence to the motto *sola scriptura*, to avoid broad concepts of authority. There exists the constant temptation to exalt the opinion of one single individual or one peculiar opinion. In the Orthodox tradition this danger

(5) *Oratio III contra Arianos*, PG 26:400.
(6) See George S. Bebis, "The Concept of Tradition in the Fathers of the Church," *Greek Orthodox Theological Review* 15:1 (1970) 39.

is, indeed, less, in that the barometer of traditional authority is always aimed away from the single event, opinion, or individual and towards the *phronema ekklesiastikon,* the *pleroma* of the Church's experience, the mystical Body of Christ, which itself encompasses Scripture by any definition.

The second characteristic of the cult enumerated by Hutten is the cult's denial of justification by grace alone. Here he champions the Reformation principle of *sola gratia* as the sine qua non for valid Christianity. To be sure, the Eastern Christian would find total dependence on God's grace an easy formula to accept. But grace in the Orthodox Church is, like Scripture, not subject to limiting definitions as such. And certainly the selective use of Pauline passages regarding grace over and against the efficacy of good works (Rom 11:6, especially), explicit in Hutten's commentary on this cultic characteristic, is unacceptable (and alien) to the East. The constant interplay between *theoria* and *praxis,* grace and good works in synergy, would disallow, for the Orthodox Christian, the artificial odds at which Western Christians place grace and salutary deeds. If by justification by grace alone one obviates, as does Hutten, the possibility of human action rising up to God and participating in grace, the very Christian experience, as the East receives it, is lost.

Between grace and good works, the Orthodox Church believes, there is a fundamental and necessary relationship dictated by personal spiritual struggle and attainment. One wise father, we are told in the *Evergetinos,* compares a person who teaches with words only, lacking deeds, to a tree with beautiful leaves which does not, however, produce fruit.[7] Another desert father tells us that we must at all times live recalling our sins,[8] which leads to humility and salvation, seemingly putting aside deeds as the essential element in spiritual life. These ostensible divergences allow for a broader definition of grace than the one proposed in the Reformation maxim *sola gratia,* for a freedom

(7) *Mikros Evergetinos* (Athens: Agion Oros, 1977), p. 30.
(8) Ibid., p. 115.

inclined toward the patristic axiom that what leads one man to perdition wins salvation for another. Grace, then, is for the Orthodox Christian the totality of God's plan for man, tailored to his individual needs, encompassing both his thoughts *and* his deeds, knowing both his heart and his actions. It neither hinders nor exalts either a man's spiritual state or his salutary deeds. The dichotomy between grace and good deeds is lost in the actualization of God's plan for any man's life.

If justification by faith is, for the Orthodox, a much more expansive formula than the one that Hutten proffers (thereby not negating the efficacy of human efforts), his grasp of salvation itself is wholly alien to the East. Professor Constantine Cavarnos has remarked, and appropriately so, that "our true ultimate end as Christians is *theosis,* deification, union with God. For this is why Christ became man, taught, suffered, was crucified, and rose from the dead—to show us by His words and deeds the way to *theosis*."[9] The patristic tradition of the East has always conceived of salvation as deification. St. Peter's New Testamental dictum that the faithful take part in the "divine nature" (2 Pet 1:4) is for the Orthodox a very definition of salvation. And while St. Maximos the Confessor stresses that salvation is given by God's grace alone, he emphasizes that God has given man the desire and will toward deification, thereby lifting his deeds up into participation in grace, in God's will.[10] Salvation (deification), St. Maximos says, is a gift given by the sacrifice of Christ, by God's grace, as a reward to man.[11] Man's actions and his deeds "earn" him, in a certain sense, the reward of deification, which in turn is the gift of God's grace. One should not, here, wish to formalize or further define these concepts and relationships, for they would lose their impact. As interacting principles, they allow for the exercise of human freedom and simultaneously for the full acknowledgment of God's singular gift of salvation to man by grace. At the same

(9) Constantine Cavarnos, "Knowing God through Icons and Hymnody," *Greek Orthodox Theological Review* 23:1 (1978) 286.

(10) PG 90:250-350 passim.

(11) Ibid., col. 637.

time, salvation as deification, as the ascendance of the mundane to divinity, necessarily makes the deeds of man (entwined as they are with the divine) efficacious—though through adoption by God. The Reformation idea of *sola gratia* as Hutten presents it does not convict the Orthodox of cultism, but convicts the motto itself of inadequacy in dealing with Orthodox Christianity.

The devaluation of the unique and singular expiatory efficacy of the person of Christ is a third characteristic of the cult, according to Professor Hutten. His formal statement of this characteristic is fully acceptable to Orthodoxy. However, there emerges in his commentary an idea that recognizing the role of other spiritual figures in man's salvation somehow devalues Christ. This idea occasions, once again, the possibility of misunderstanding or dismissing Orthodox precepts as cultic; for, indeed, while fully adhering to the belief that *only* through the redemptive sacrifice of Christ is man saved, the Orthodox Church recognizes the effectiveness of and need for intercession before Christ by the saints and most especially by the Theotokos, the Virgin Mother of God. But, as we shall see subsequently, the recognition of intercessory powers is not a devaluation of Christ, but rather a full application of his redemptive powers, an expansive awareness of the transforming effect of his sacrifice on his own mother and on the saints. One would expect nothing less from the Church which is heir to the Christological synods, which championed the basic formulations of Christ's nature, work, and sacrifice, to which formulation even Hutten's Reformed tradition owes a great debt for its Christology—a Christology which, in its Reformed interpretation, has come to have limitations in definition too great to allow it to serve as the absolute criterion by which another tradition is pronounced genuine or cultic.

It is a sad and grievous thing that the devotion of the Eastern Church to the Virgin Mary is so often misunderstood by Western Protestants, for it is par excellence a Christological devotion. First, we can agree with the trenchant observations of Jaroslav Pelikan that the Mariological doctrines of the Orthodox Church have as their "principal locus" liturgical worship; even their dogmatic articulation arose out of worship and devotion.[12] It was in the very liturgies (notably those of Sts. Basil and Chrysostom), in which Christ is "invisibly present" (Liturgy of Chrysostom), that the intercession of Mary was encountered. Her intercession in the mystical presence of Christ (reflected in traditional iconography, where the lone figure of the Theotokos, without the image of Christ, is very rare) emphasizes that this intercession is Christological in essence and in function, an integral part of the believer's reception of Christ. Secondly, since this intercession is perfectly in keeping with scriptural references to the intercession (prayers) of the righteous as helpful to man, there is not a basic extrascriptural source for Orthodox Mariology. It is both scriptural and Christocentric. And finally, because the birth of Christ to the Virgin Mother of God, as St. Maximos the Confessor has written, symbolizes the birth of Christ in an unbodily way *(asomatos)* in the believer, taking part, as he does, in the divine nature (2 Pet 1:4), the Theotokos is the very core of man's acquisition of Christ's redemptive promise.[13] It is, no doubt, because of the immediacy of the Virgin Mary's image in man's realization of the salvation offered in Christ that the early Church so naturally and so spontaneously accepted Mariology, not as a usurpation of the Lord's singular expiatory significance, but as a participation in and expression of that redemption.

Too often Protestants also assume that the so-called "cults of the saints" are, in the Eastern Church, wrought with the non-Christocentric abuses that one sometimes finds in Roman Catholic hagiolatry. This is unfortunate, for in actuality the Eastern Orthodox veneration of saints is a direct veneration of Christ himself. Sainthood is best defined as deification, i.e., union with Christ. Father Kallistos (Timothy) Ware superbly expresses this truth in his incisive assertion that, "if the saints are so-called, it is because they participate in the sanctity of

---

(12) Jaroslav Pelikan, *The Spirit of Eastern Christendom (600-1700)* (Chicago: University of Chicago Press, 1974), p. 139.

(13) See above, chapter 6.

God—because they have been 'deified,' becoming 'gods by Grace.' 'Christs in Jesus Christ.' '"[14] One notices in this astounding statement the absence of the special position of mediation so carefully formalized in Latin hagiolatry, and senses immediately that the Orthodox view of sainthood is closely connected with Christology, soteriology, and, as we have suggested above, Mariology as well. Any thought of eastern veneration of saints as detracting from the expiatory singularity of Christ's sacrifice seems far-fetched, even to the least objective of observers. And though this formulation of the Eastern Church's tradition with regard to saints is neither new nor uniquely stated here, it goes repeatedly unheeded by Protestant observers. It is this frequent disregard which can lead to misunderstanding and to misstatement of the supremely Christocentric nature of the Orthodox witness.

The last major characteristic of the cult offered by Hutten that we wish to consider is that of the exclusivity of the group as a community of the saved. Using a broad definition of the Church catholic, Hutten opines that any group that lays claim to exclusive truth is cultic. Certainly one is prompted to agree that very restrictive definitions of the Church that discourage by their formulation Christian witness and evangelical mission are cultic, if not abhorrent. But at the same time, it would be naive, indeed, to imagine that Scripture and church tradition do not identify true members of the Body of Christ as a select group in possession, not only of truth, but of the uniqueness of a new life. Moreover, it is curious that Professor Hutten decries as cultic any "corner" on the truth, while at the same time denying the Christianity of those who do not share his precisely stated Reformed theological requisites. No doubt this curiosity emerges only in critical focus and perhaps by overstatement, but the danger for the Orthodox Christian, who thinks of himself in many ways as expressing an exclusive truth, is implicit.

As a rejoinder to Professor Hutten's objection to an exclu-

---

(14) Timothy Ware, "The Communion of Saints," in A. J. Philippou, ed., *The Orthodox Ethos* (Oxford, 1964), p. 143.

109

sivistic ecclesiastical stance, we might address the claims of the Eastern Orthodox Church with some care. It must, at the outset, be understood that Orthodox, perhaps as in no other tradition, have a compelling claim to exclusivity as the Church of Christ. The early Church, in the great and holy ecumenical synods, in which the basic tenets of Christian doctrine accepted by almost all traditions were defined, was preponderantly an Eastern Church. The synods themselves were overwhelmingly attended by bishops of the eastern sees. And the earliest extant liturgical traditions are eastern. These facts, then, bespeak the historical dimension in which the Eastern Orthodox Church conceives of her exclusivity. And because she sees herself, in this historical context, as the very Ark of Salvation, the very Church of Christ, she also proclaims herself the exclusive community of the saved. Nowhere in traditional ecclesiological statements has the Orthodox Church known herself as anything else. But neither has the Church ever failed to know this exclusivity as an historical manifestation, not as some institutional trait; nor has she separated this claim from her foundation in Christ, by which fact she is compelled to announce the Gospel to all men and to pronounce an exclusivity open to all.

At another level, Hutten neglects the fact that claims to exclusivity carry with them responsibilities that belie the arrogance of the cultic self-appropriation of truth. It is not so much exclusivity that effects a cultic trait, but the source and effect of that supposed exclusivity. As we have noted, an exclusivity traced essentially to Christ demands, paradoxically, an open attitude toward others. At the same time, it demands humility and love. In considering itself the Church of Christ, the Orthodox Church simultaneously recognizes its responsibility to express this exclusivity in acts of love toward all men, regardless of their beliefs, and to do so always with humility. To express an exclusive truth which one is called upon to promulgate and to actualize in his life is not, then, necessarily something cultic or negative. Thus it is that we find St. Kosmas Aitolos, deeply committed to the exclusive claims to primacy of the Orthodox Church, warning that it is on the wings of humility and love

110

only that the Christian soars into paradise.[15] Exclusivity is quite obviously not always un-Christian and arrogant.

Lastly, one must not imagine that the Orthodox claims to exclusive possession of the truth are without pragmatic ramifications. The Orthodox view of the Church is not solely institutional. St. Serafim of Sarov is well known for his characterization of Christian practices as indispensable means to the end of spiritual attainment, but not ends in themselves.[16] In a limited sense we can say that the Church, too, is a vessel, that it serves the end of carrying man into the safe harbor of salvation, of deifying man and of witnessing the divine in the world. She can hold up as the accomplishment of this task the many God-bearing fathers who have entered into the "divine nature." She can lay before the world the many grace-filled relics of their ascent. She can offer up in sacrifice the lifegiving mysteries which any man can inwardly touch, feel, and experience. The Church can set forth the Christian goal, a path (a means to an end), and can witness the fact that holy saints have attained that end by the same means which the Church has established. A claim to exclusivity in such an instance is not so much a claim to possession as it is an inviting offer to accept a "tried and true" road.

Let us expand further on this idea of the Church as a guide. Envision life as *peregrinatio,* as a wandering pilgrimage through a deep and dark forest. Let us see the Church as offering a path cut through the forest to the Lifegiving Fountain of pure waters in the region of light beyond the dark forest. Through the divine mysteries, those traveling this path are renewed and encourged by grace-filled water brought from the Fountain to nourish them on their journey. But along this dark road are many dangerous pitfalls and stumbling blocks. These, though unseen in the darkness, are marked by roadsigns of tradition left by the saints who have successfully trodden this dark path. These roadsigns, if accepted with inner faith by the traveler, are his protection and

(15) Constantine Cavarnos, *St. Cosmas Aitolos* (Belmont, Mass.: Institute for Byzantine and Modern Greek Studies, 1971), p. 49.

(16) See Vladimir Lossky, *The Mystical Theology of the Eastern Church* (London: James Clarke and Co., 1957), p. 196.

salvation from fatal falls. Surrounded by darkness on all sides, out of which are heard the demonic calls of every peril, enticing the traveler to stop his journey and refresh himself with the poisonous waters available along the roadside, the path is a fearful one. In this pilgrimage, imagine what peril would await the traveler if he decided to trudge out into the darkness in search of a shorter, easier, or more appealing path. And imagine what the Church would be if, ignoring those whom she has surely guided to the Lifegiving Fountain, she were to say, "Yes, there are other roads," allowing the traveler to find himself in darkness. And even if there were other roads, would it be responsible to send a weary, weak traveler out seeking them in peril, taking from him the nourishment of her mysteries and the benefit of the perfect guideposts established on the much-trodden path of tradition? Certainly not. Exclusivity becomes not an abstract, institutional claim, but an absolute condition for survival. It is not characteristic of the cult only, but, in its true application, of responsible Christian guidance, of the critical need to keep man on the safe road to spiritual attainment, and away from the dangers of passing from path to path, going nowhere, or perhaps taking to a road that has no destination. Exclusivity is, in essence, a pragmatic necessity.

From our discussion it is evident that Professor Hutten's essentially theological characterization of the cult is inadequate to deal with the expansive theological notions of the Eastern Orthodox witness.

INDEX

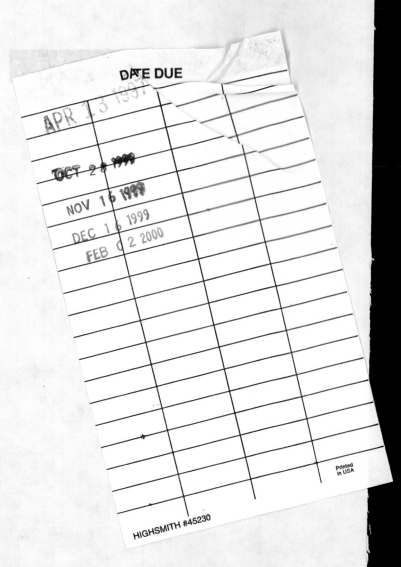

DATE DUE

APR 1 3 1997

OCT 2 8 1999

NOV 1 6 1999

DEC 1 6 1999

FEB 0 2 2000

Printed
In USA

HIGHSMITH #45230